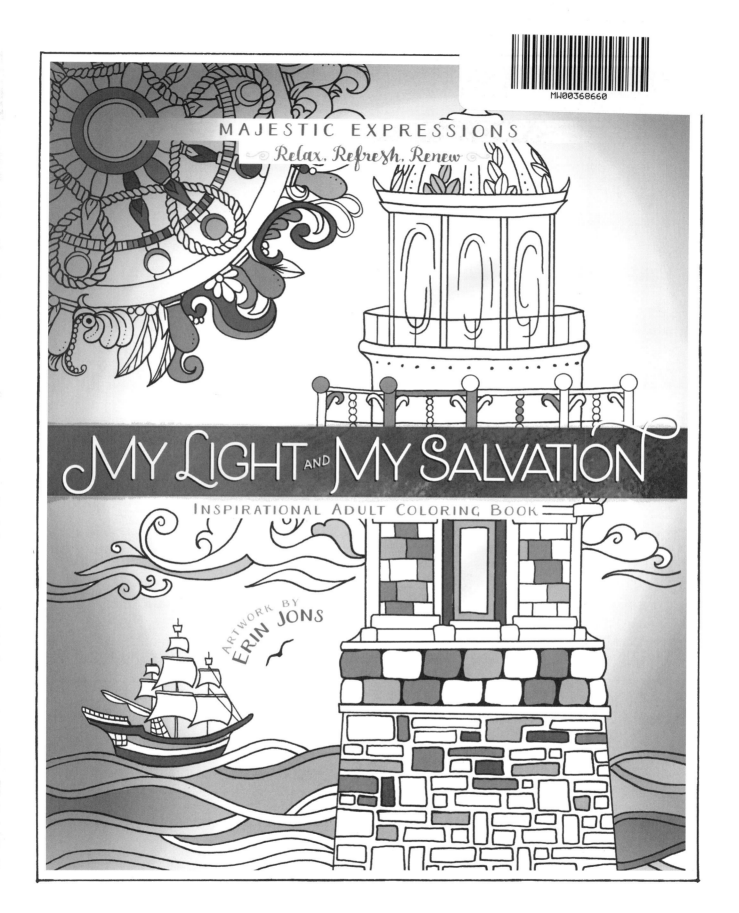

MAJESTIC EXPRESSIONS
Relax, Refresh, Renew

MY LIGHT AND MY SALVATION

INSPIRATIONAL ADULT COLORING BOOK

ARTWORK BY
ERIN JONS

BroadStreet
PUBLISHING

BroadStreet Publishing Group LLC
Racine, Wisconsin, USA
Broadstreetpublishing.com

MAJESTIC EXPRESSIONS

My Light and My Salvation

© 2016 by BroadStreet Publishing

ISBN 978-1-4245-5248-1

Artwork by Erin Jons.

Cover design by Chris Garborg | garborgdesign.com
Compiled and edited by Michelle Winger | literallyprecise.com

Printed in the United States of America.

16 17 18 19 20 21 22   7 6 5 4 3 2 1

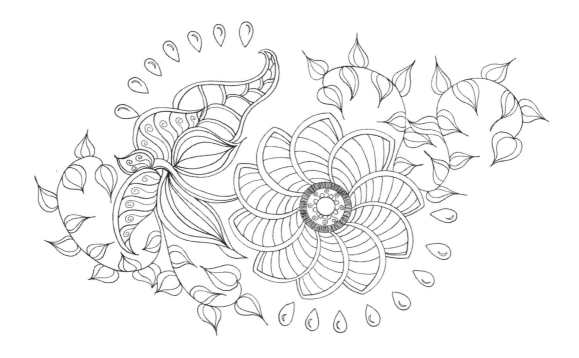

ABOUT THE ILLUSTRATOR

ERIN JONS is a self-taught artist who enjoys the intricacies of creativity. Her relationship with paper and ink began in 1998 as she drew, sketched, and doodled her way through the trials of high school lectures. This relationship has continued in the form of portraits, theatrical set design, and drawing countless coloring pages for her own children. She is humbled and delighted to see her art mingle with God's precious and powerful Word, and prays that time spent with each page will reveal a glimpse of the beauty of Jesus. Erin is happily married with five children in Northern Idaho.

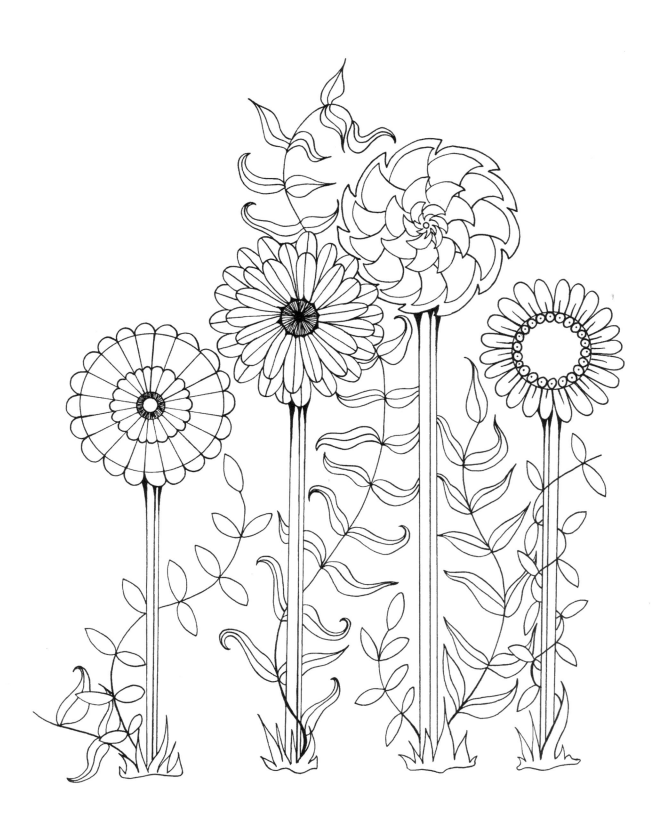

INTRODUCTION

WHY ADULT COLORING BOOKS?

There is plenty of research that shows coloring to be an effective stress reducer. Maybe you picked up this book because you've heard the hype and you're curious. Perhaps you've been looking for a way to relax. Or, if you're like many others we've encountered, you've been looking for a good excuse to color since you "grew up" and coloring books were no longer an acceptable hobby. Over the years, you may have found yourself eager to babysit kids who were fond of coloring, or maybe you have children or grandchildren of your own that need your help filling in the pages of their coloring books.

Finally you hold in your hand your very own adult coloring book. And you have every reason you need to sit down and color. You have entered a stress-free zone. There's no wrong way to color. If you want the grass to be blue and the sky to be green, go right ahead. If you only want to color a portion of a picture, do it. Crayons? Coloring pencils? Markers? It's your choice. This is your book, and this is your time.

Let's take it a step further. While coloring may be a great distraction from all you have going on, the best way to find lasting peace is to spend time with your Creator. As you fill these intricately designed illustrations with the beauty of color, dwell on the richness of his Word, the faithfulness of his character, and the depth of his love for you.

"I HAVE TOLD YOU THESE THINGS, SO THAT IN ME YOU MAY HAVE PEACE.
IN THIS WORLD YOU WILL HAVE TROUBLE.
BUT TAKE HEART! I HAVE OVERCOME THE WORLD."
JOHN 16:33 NIV

Happy coloring!

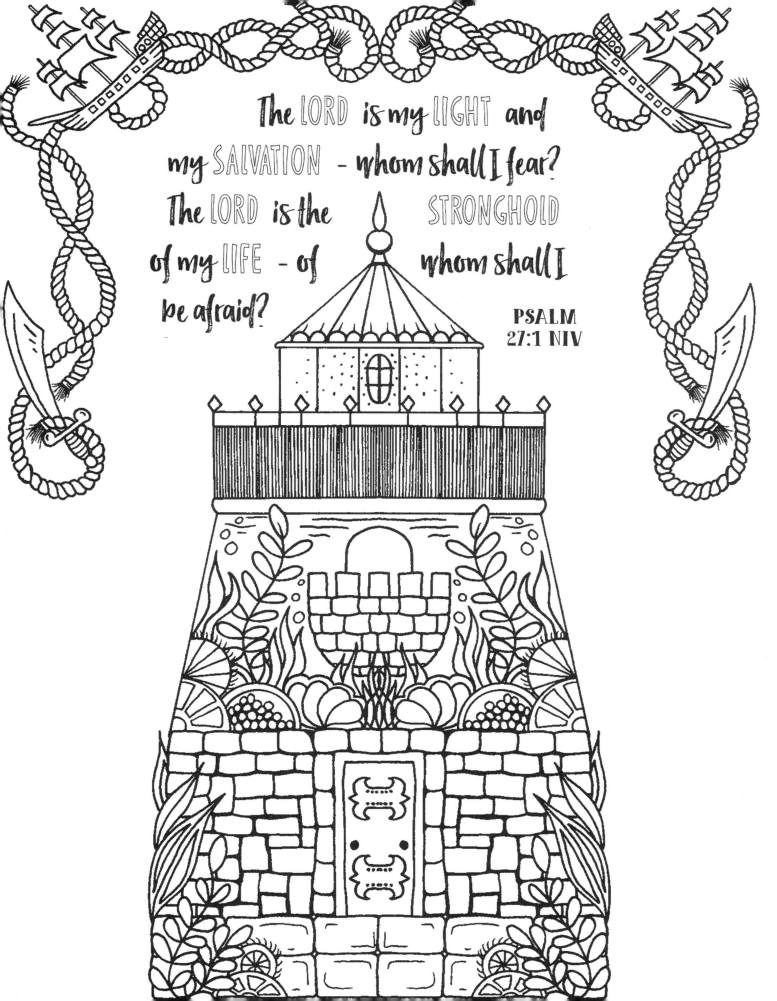

The LORD is my LIGHT and my SALVATION - whom shall I fear? The LORD is the STRONGHOLD of my LIFE - of whom shall I be afraid?

PSALM 27:1 NIV

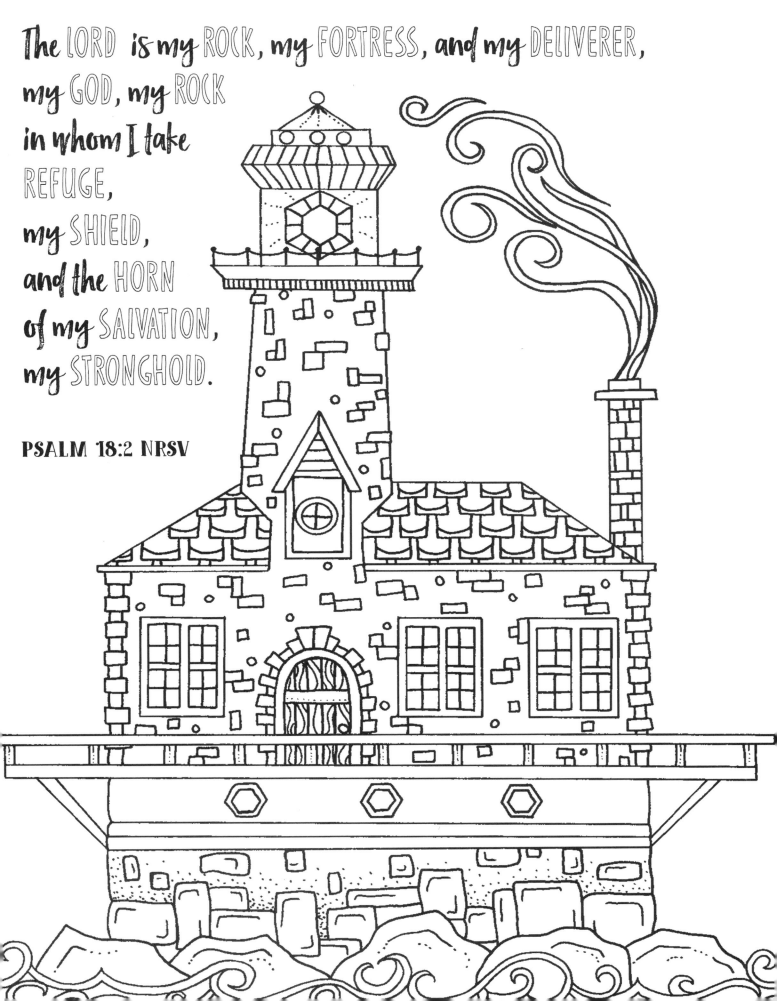

The LORD is my ROCK, my FORTRESS, and my DELIVERER, my GOD, my ROCK in whom I take REFUGE, my SHIELD, and the HORN of my SALVATION, my STRONGHOLD.

PSALM 18:2 NRSV

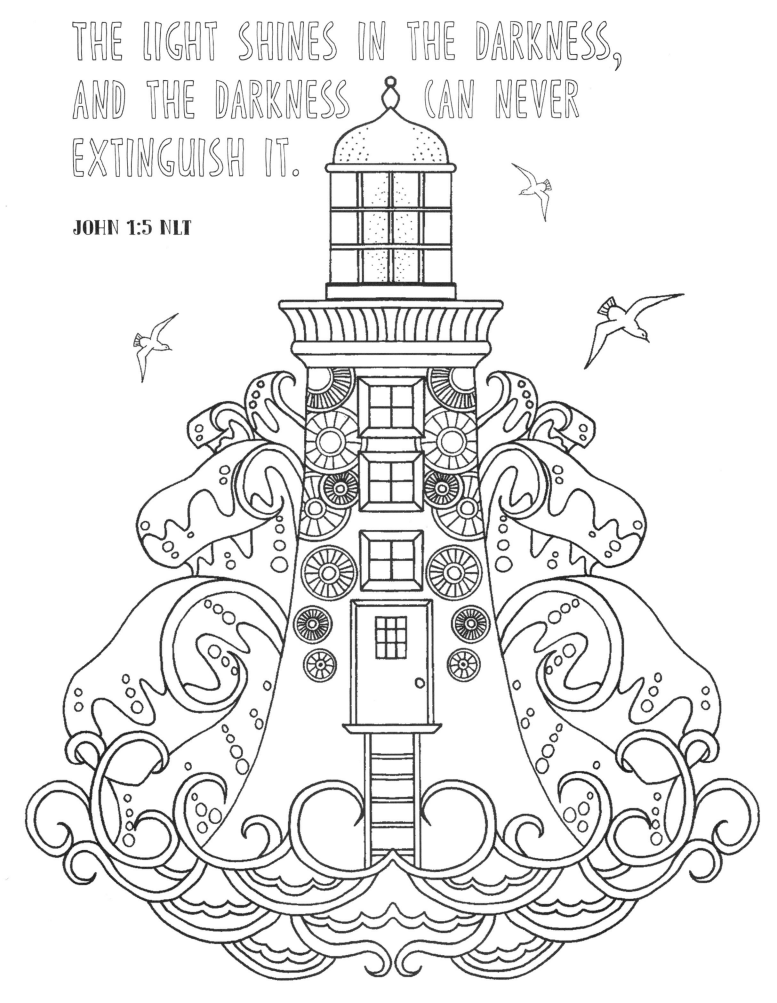

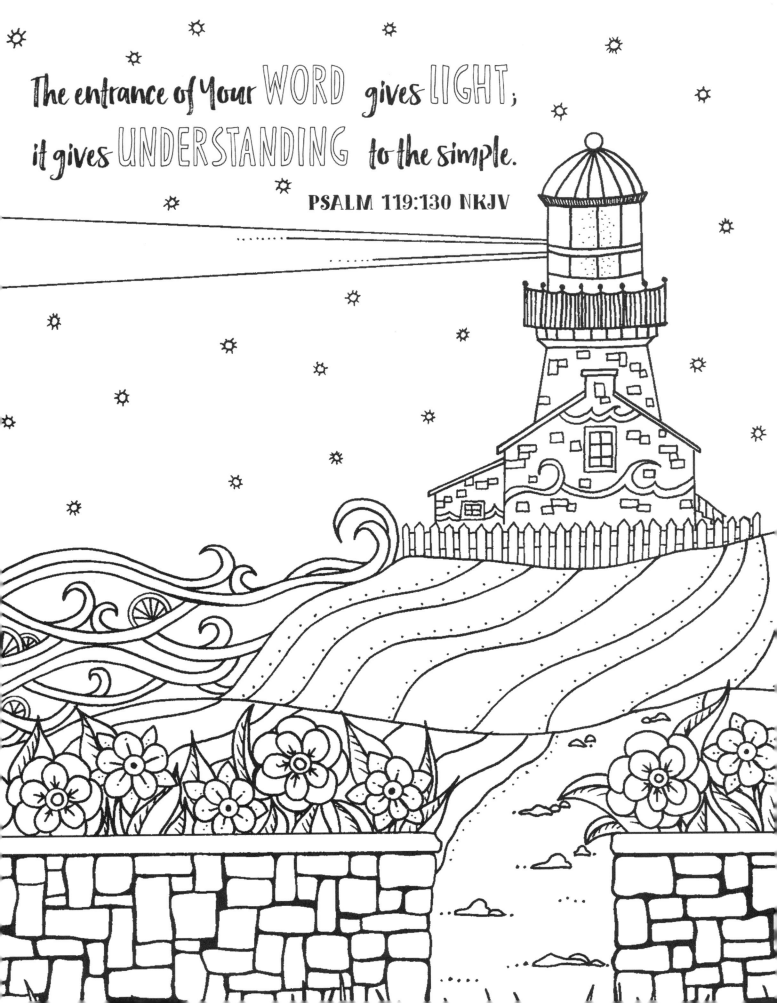

The entrance of Your WORD gives LIGHT; it gives UNDERSTANDING to the simple.

PSALM 119:130 NKJV

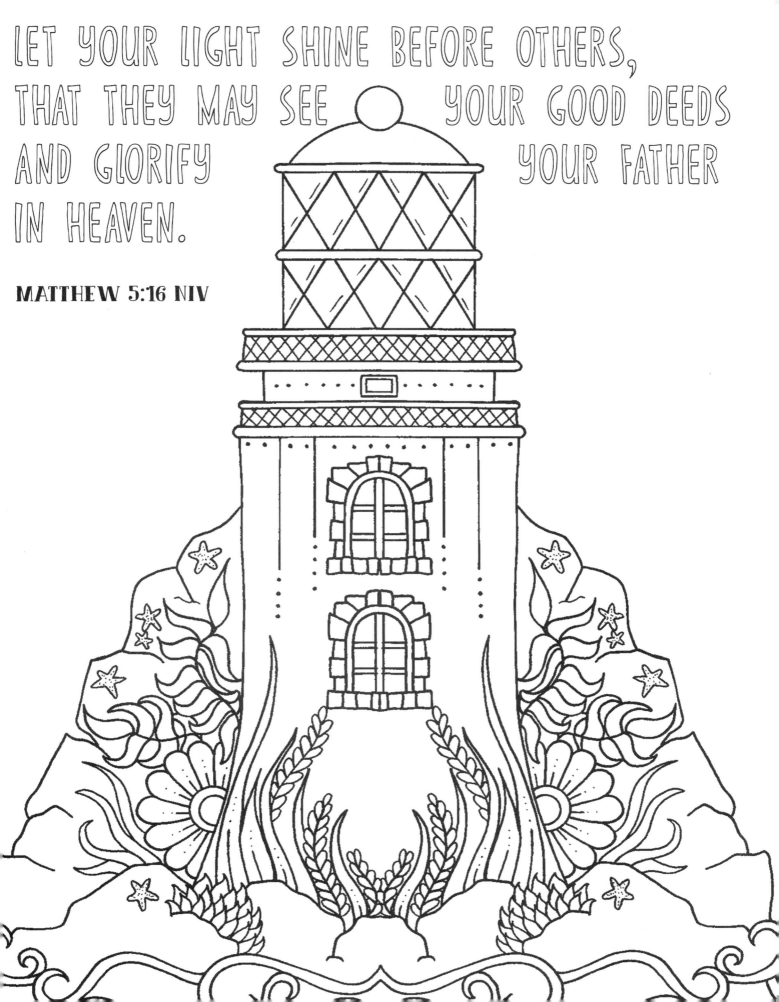

LET YOUR LIGHT SHINE BEFORE OTHERS,
THAT THEY MAY SEE YOUR GOOD DEEDS
AND GLORIFY YOUR FATHER
IN HEAVEN.

MATTHEW 5:16 NIV

GOD HAS RESCUED ME FROM THE GRAVE, AND NOW MY LIFE IS FILLED WITH LIGHT.

JOB 33:28 NLT

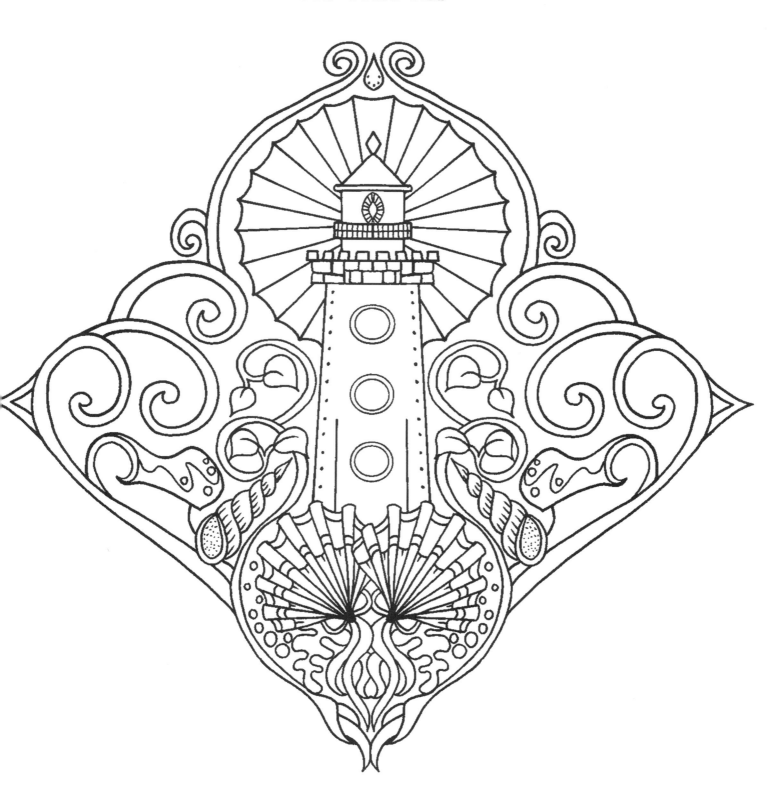

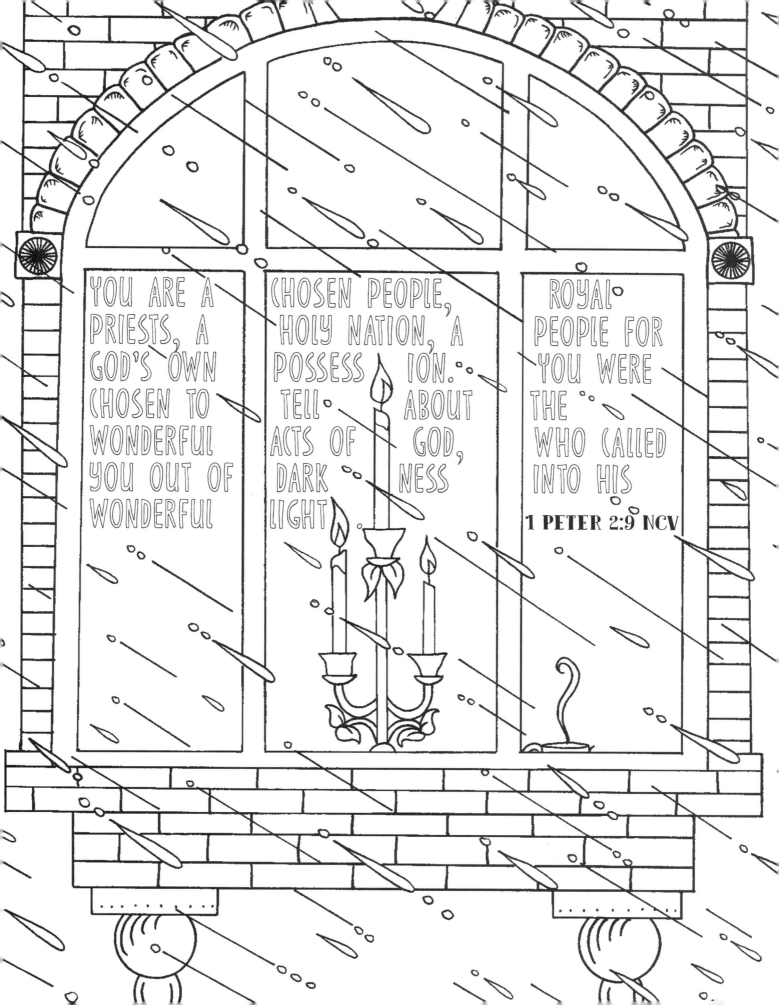

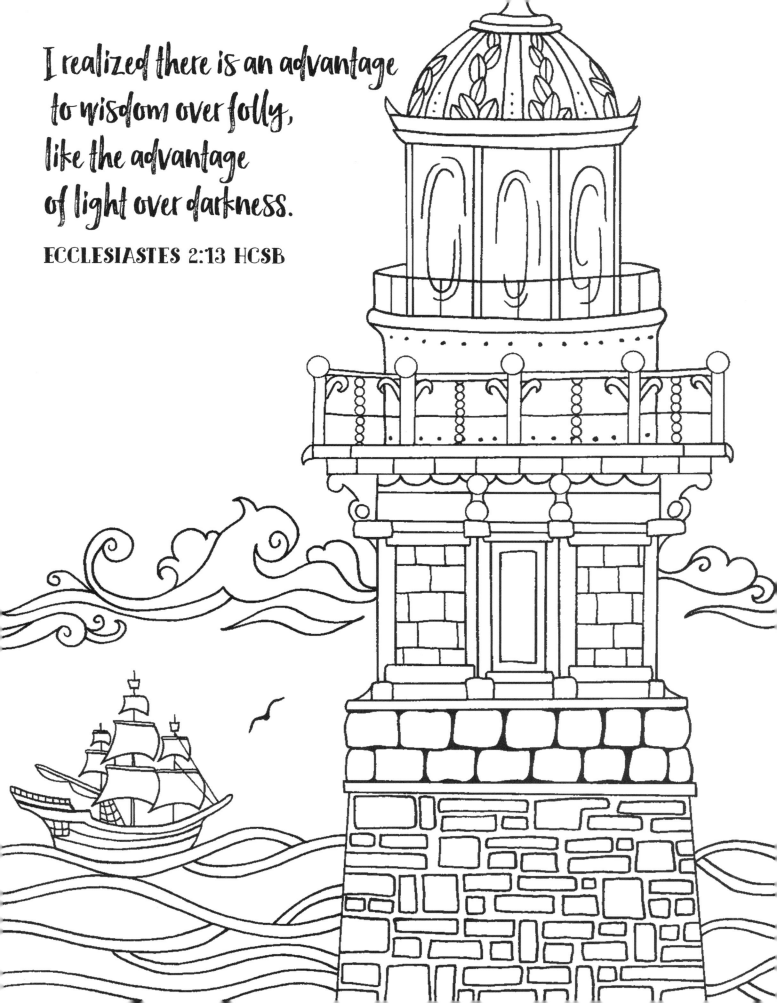

I realized there is an advantage
to wisdom over folly,
like the advantage
of light over darkness.

ECCLESIASTES 2:13 HCSB

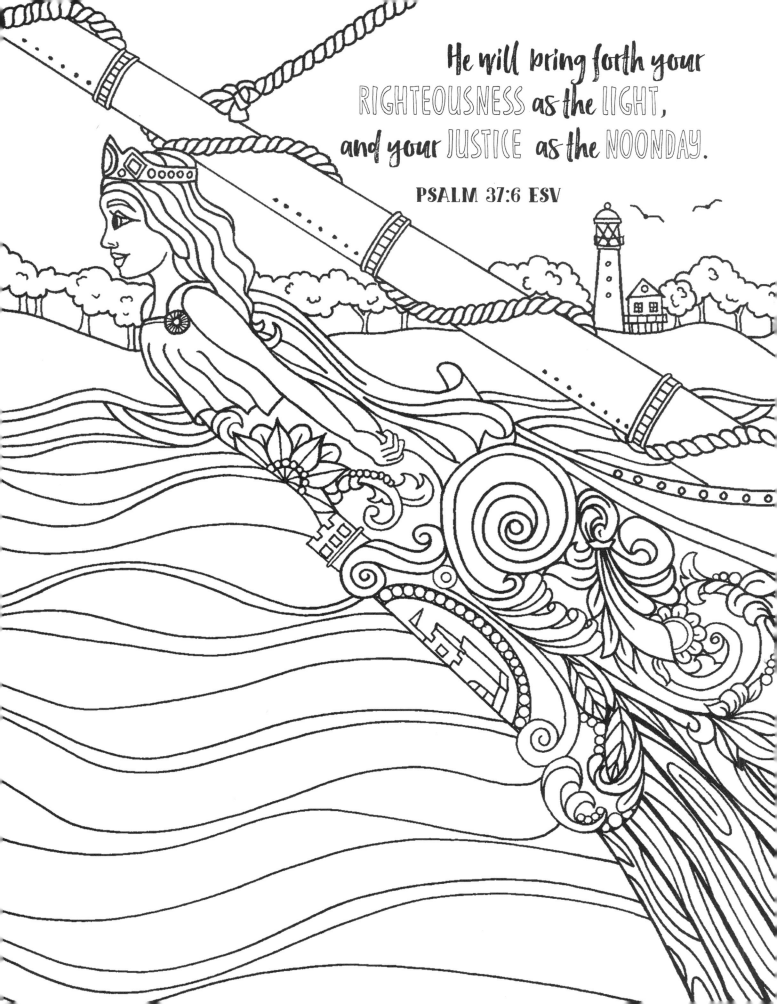

He will bring forth your RIGHTEOUSNESS as the LIGHT, and your JUSTICE as the NOONDAY.

PSALM 37:6 ESV

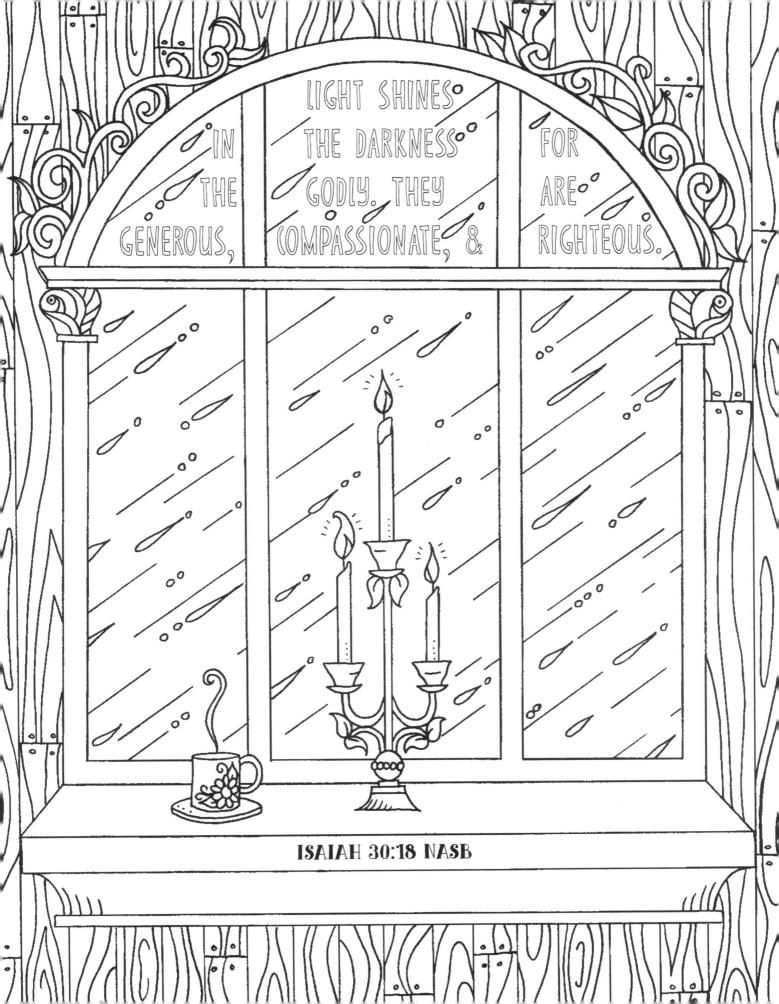

LIGHT SHINES
IN THE DARKNESS
THE GODLY. THEY FOR
GENEROUS, COMPASSIONATE, & RIGHTEOUS.

ISAIAH 30:18 NASB

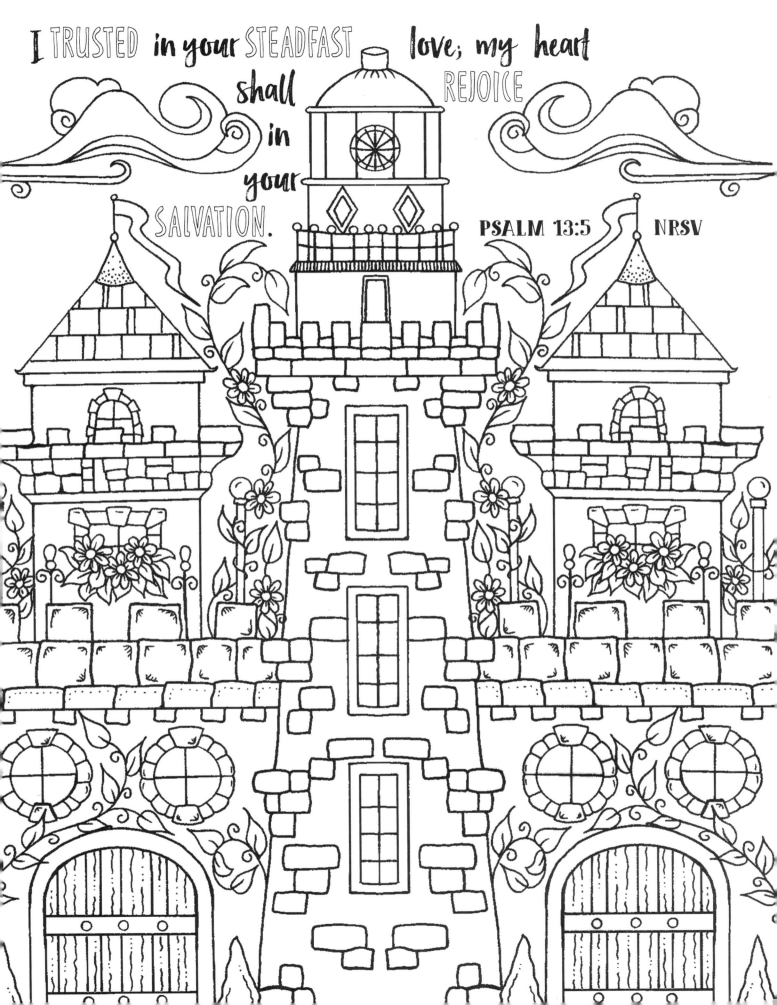

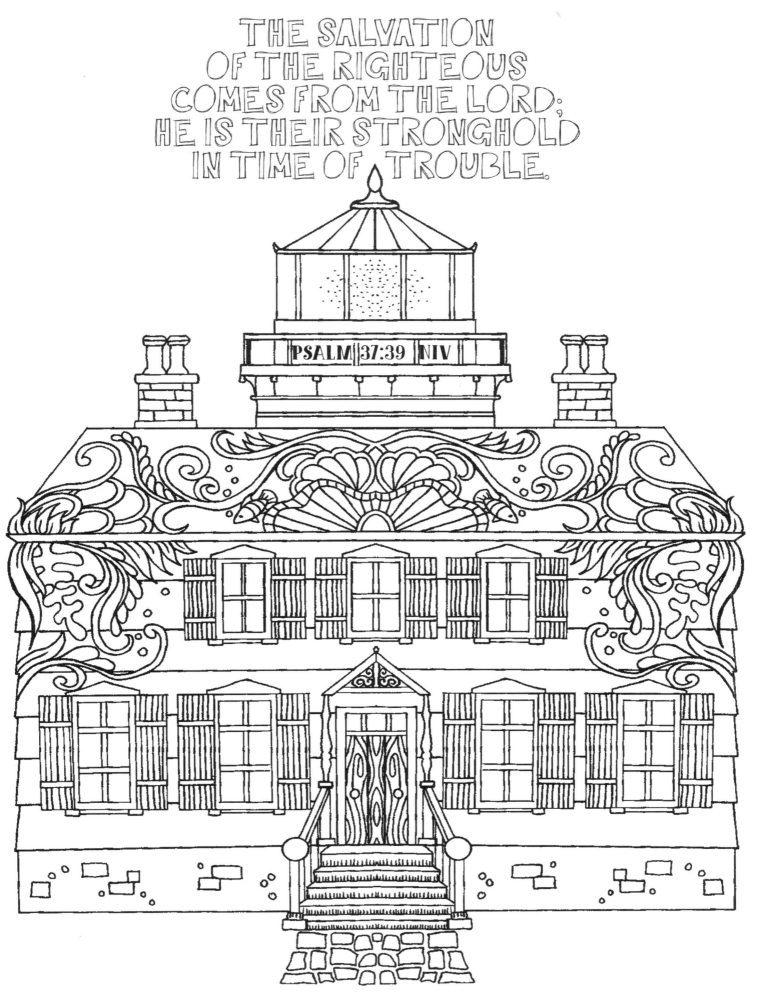

GOD IS LIGHT;

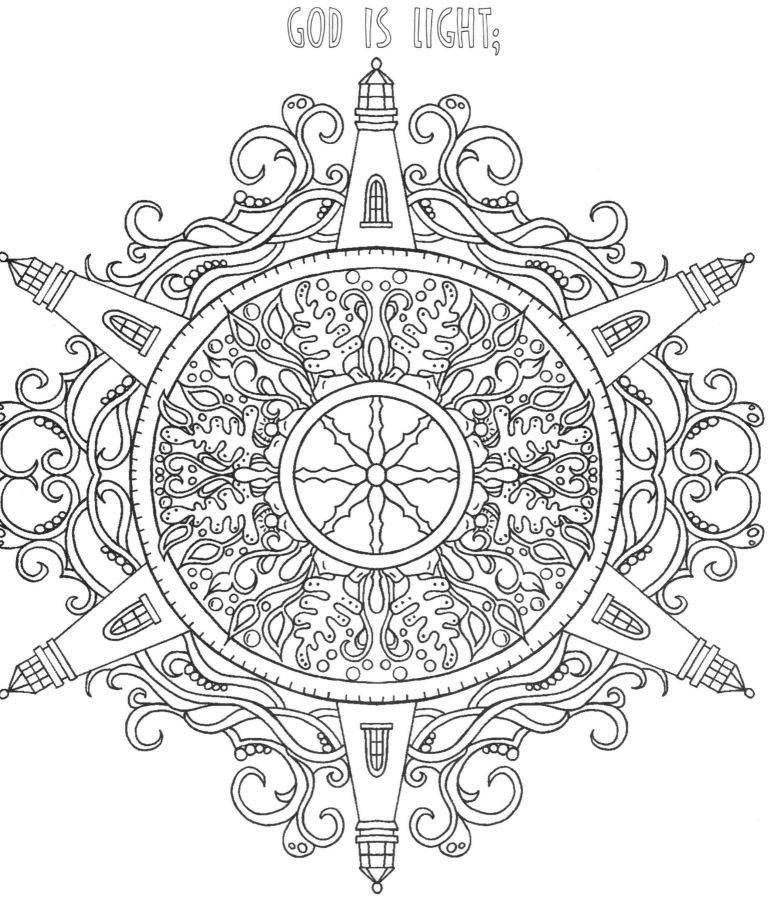

IN HIM THERE IS NO DARKNESS AT ALL.
1 JOHN 1:5 NIV

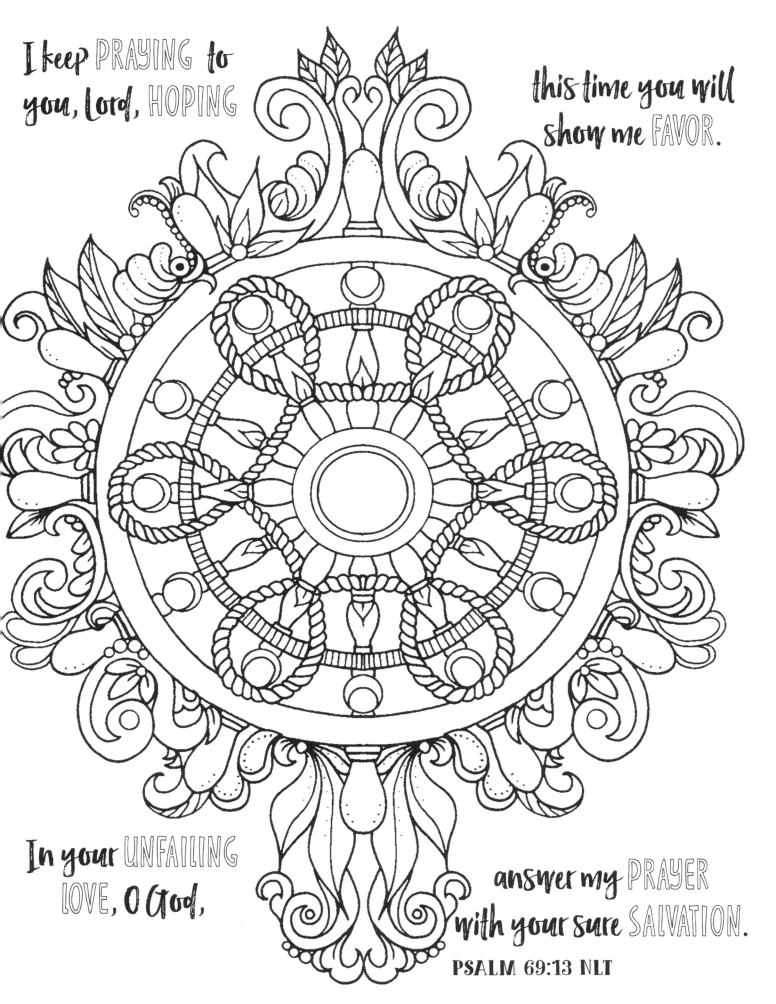

I keep PRAYING to you, Lord, HOPING

this time you will show me FAVOR.

In your UNFAILING LOVE, O God,

answer my PRAYER with your sure SALVATION.

PSALM 69:13 NLT

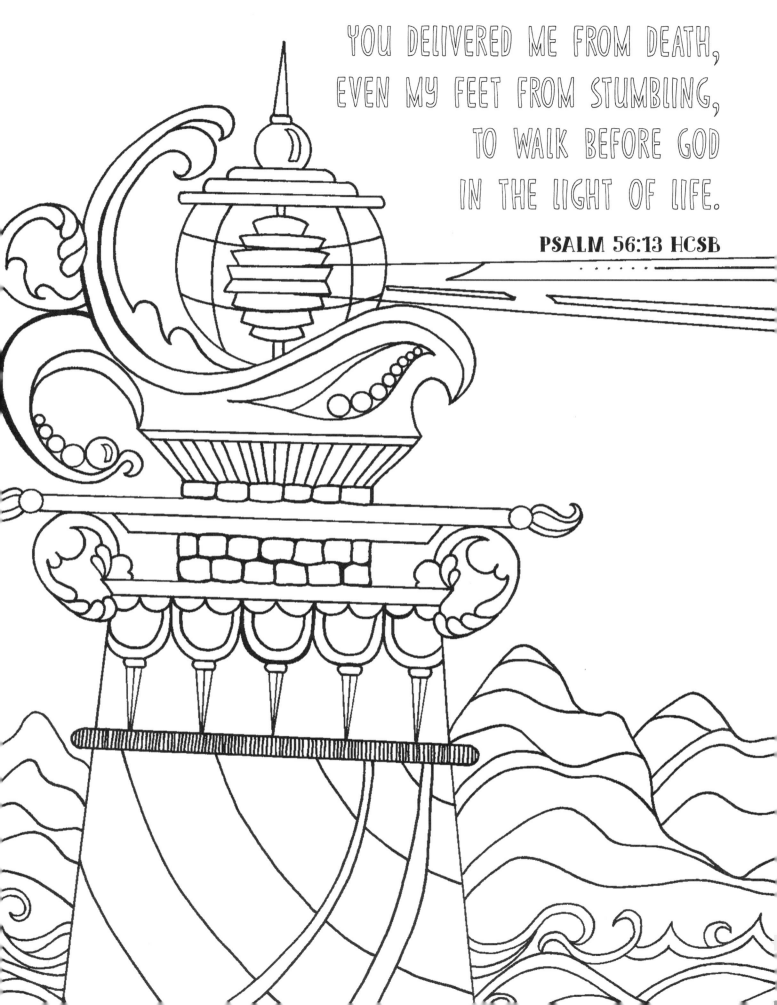

YOU DELIVERED ME FROM DEATH,
EVEN MY FEET FROM STUMBLING,
TO WALK BEFORE GOD
IN THE LIGHT OF LIFE.

PSALM 56:13 HCSB

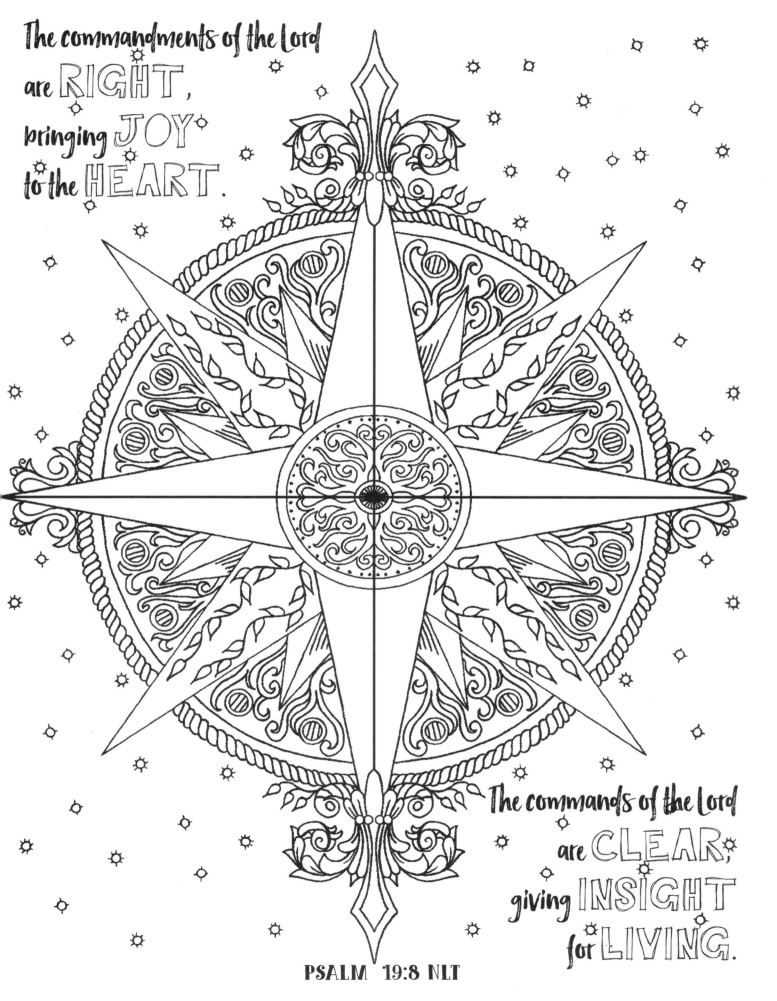

The commandments of the Lord are RIGHT, bringing JOY to the HEART.

The commands of the Lord are CLEAR, giving INSIGHT for LIVING.

PSALM 19:8 NLT

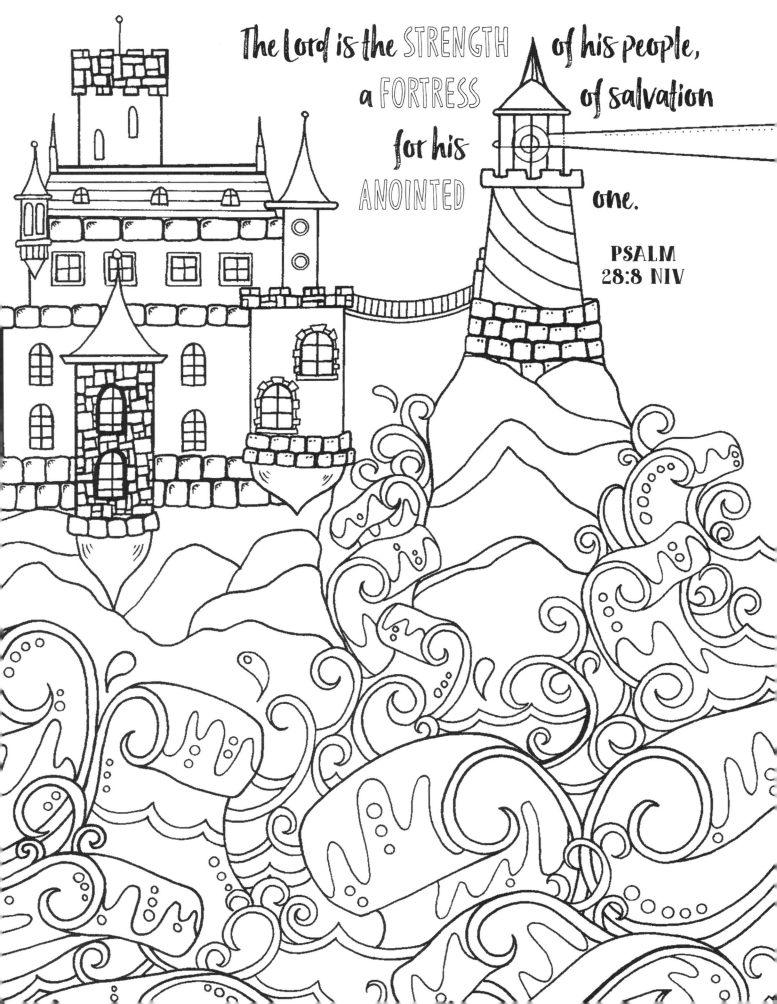

The Lord is the STRENGTH of his people, a FORTRESS for his ANOINTED one, of salvation.

PSALM 28:8 NIV

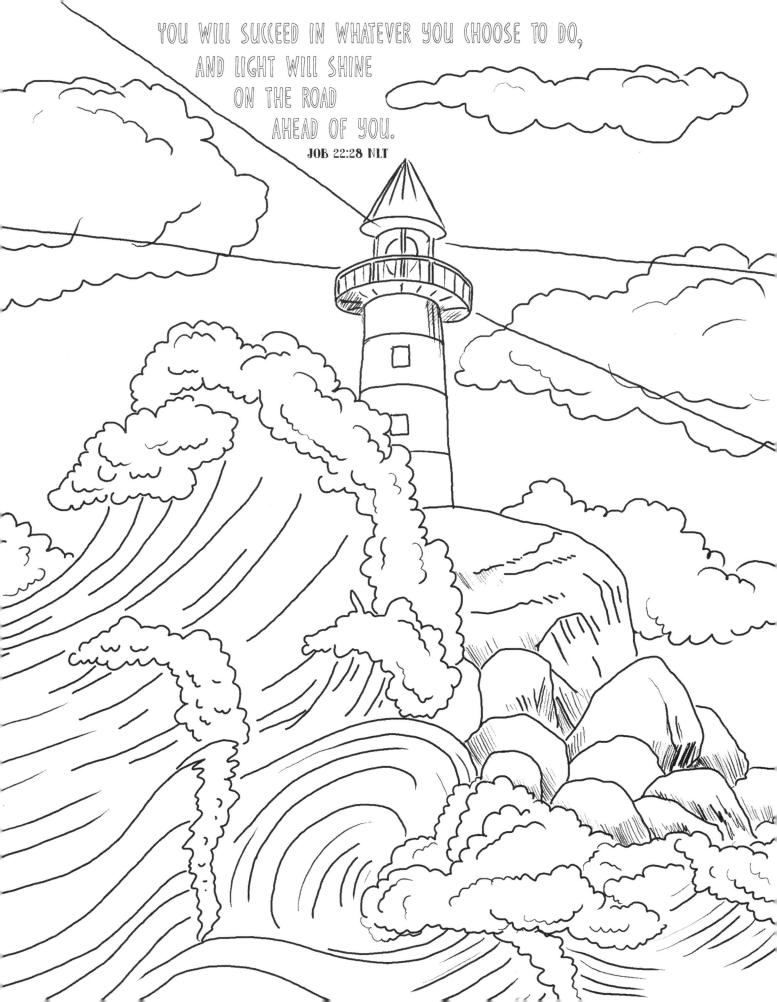

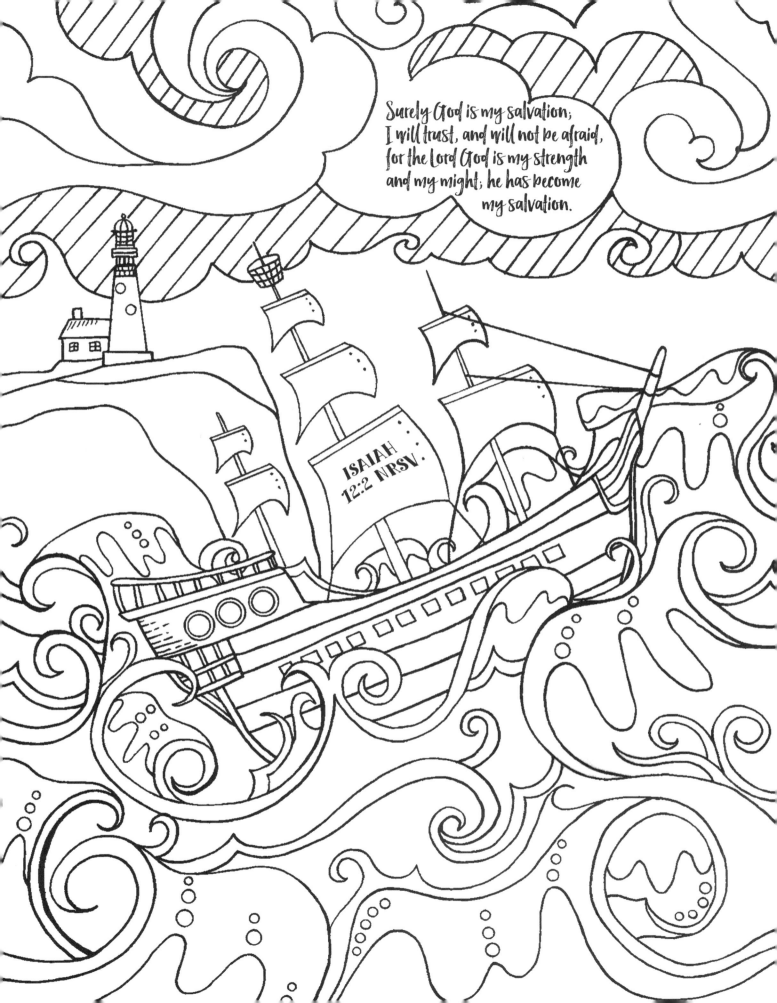

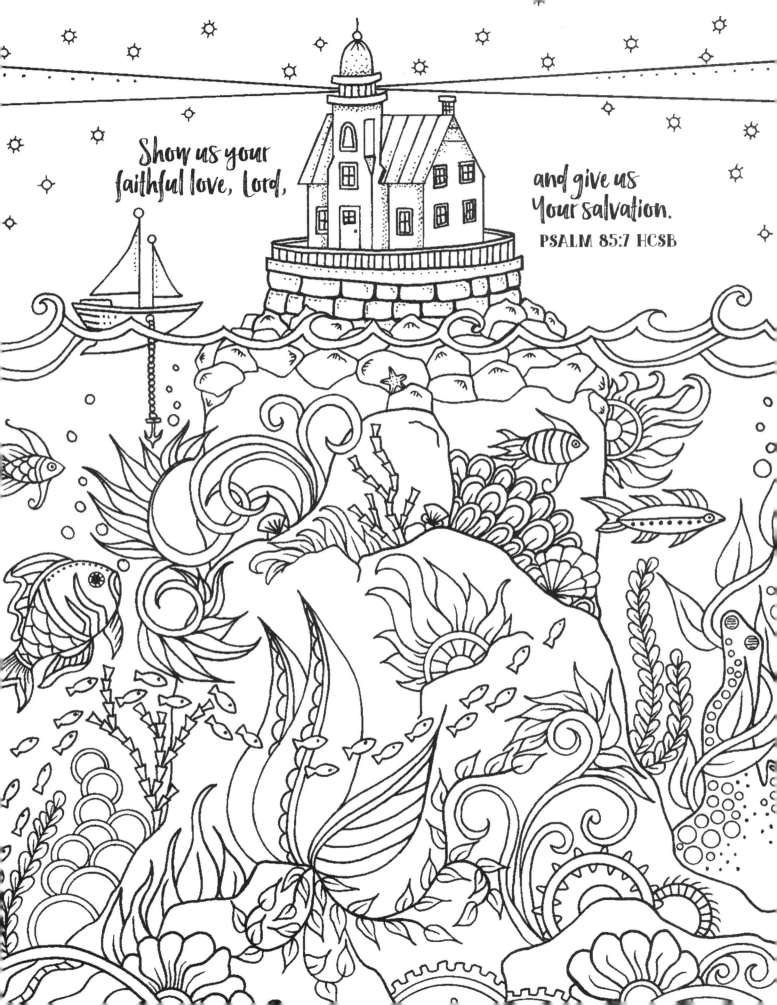

Show us your faithful love, Lord, and give us Your salvation.

PSALM 85:7 HCSB

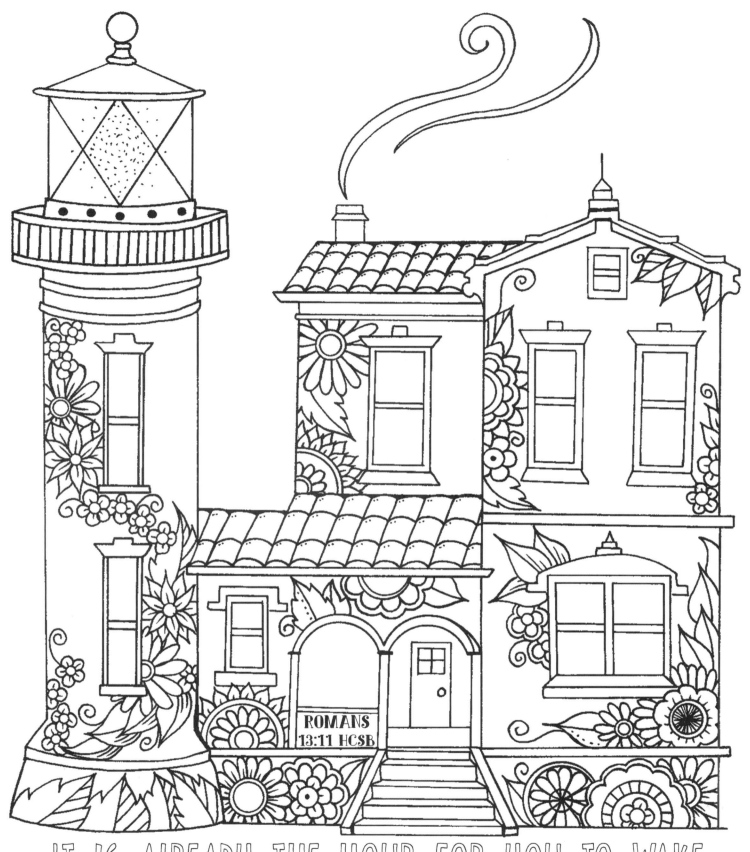

ROMANS
13:11 HCSB

IT IS ALREADY THE HOUR FOR YOU TO WAKE
UP FROM SLEEP, FOR NOW OUR SALVATION
IS NEARER THAN WHEN WE FIRST BELIEVED.

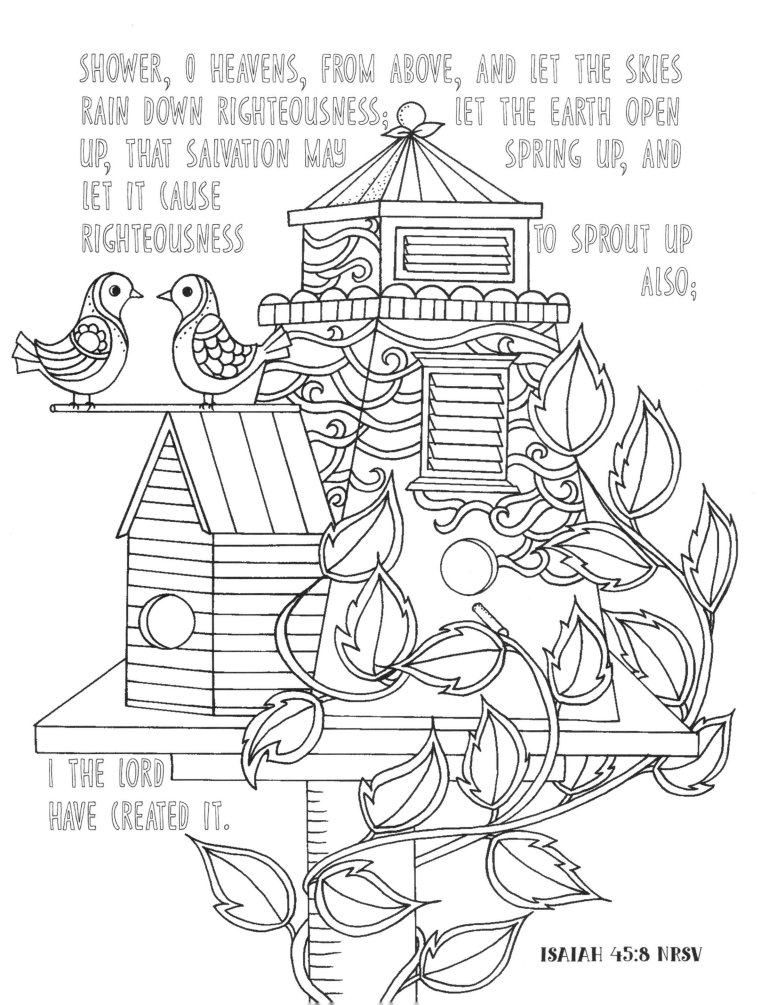

THE LORD HAS MADE
HIS SALVATION KNOWN
AND REVEALED HIS
RIGHTEOUSNESS
TO THE NATIONS.

PSALM 98:2 NIV

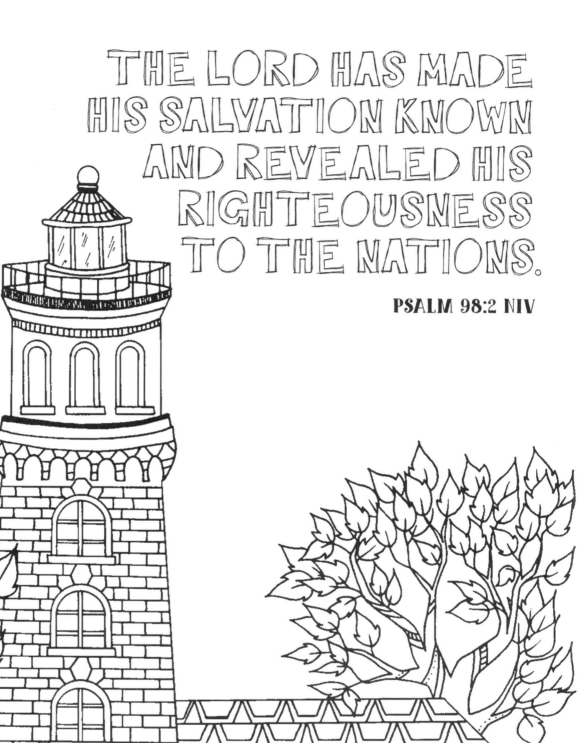

THERE IS SALVATION IN NO ONE ELSE! GOD HAS GIVEN NO OTHER NAME UNDER HEAVEN BY WHICH WE MUST BE SAVED.

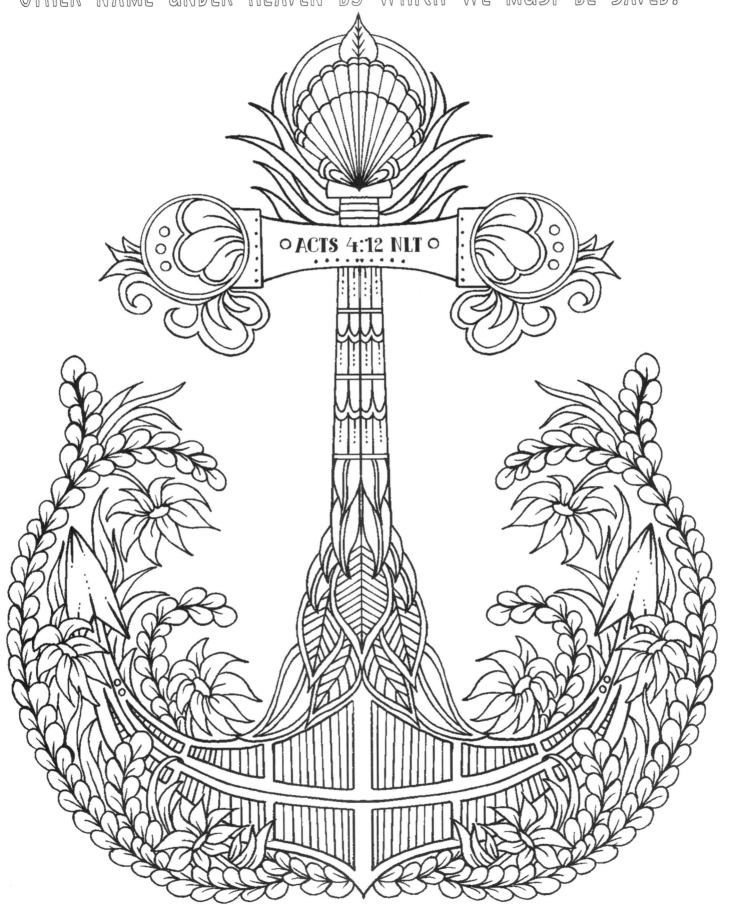

ACTS 4:12 NLT

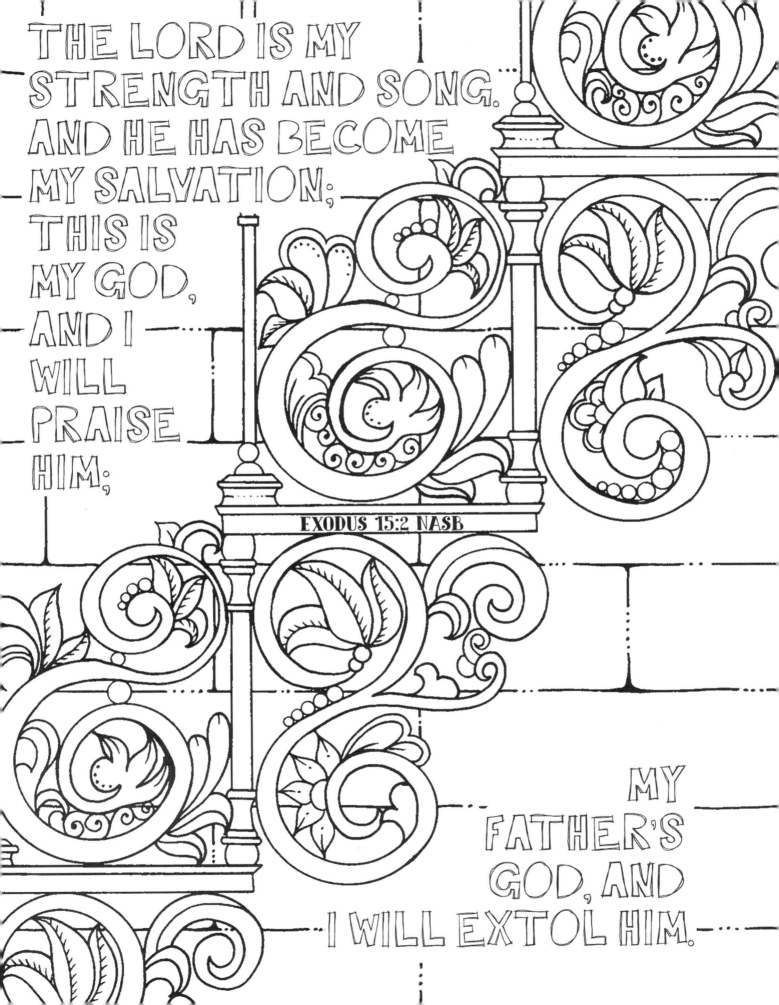

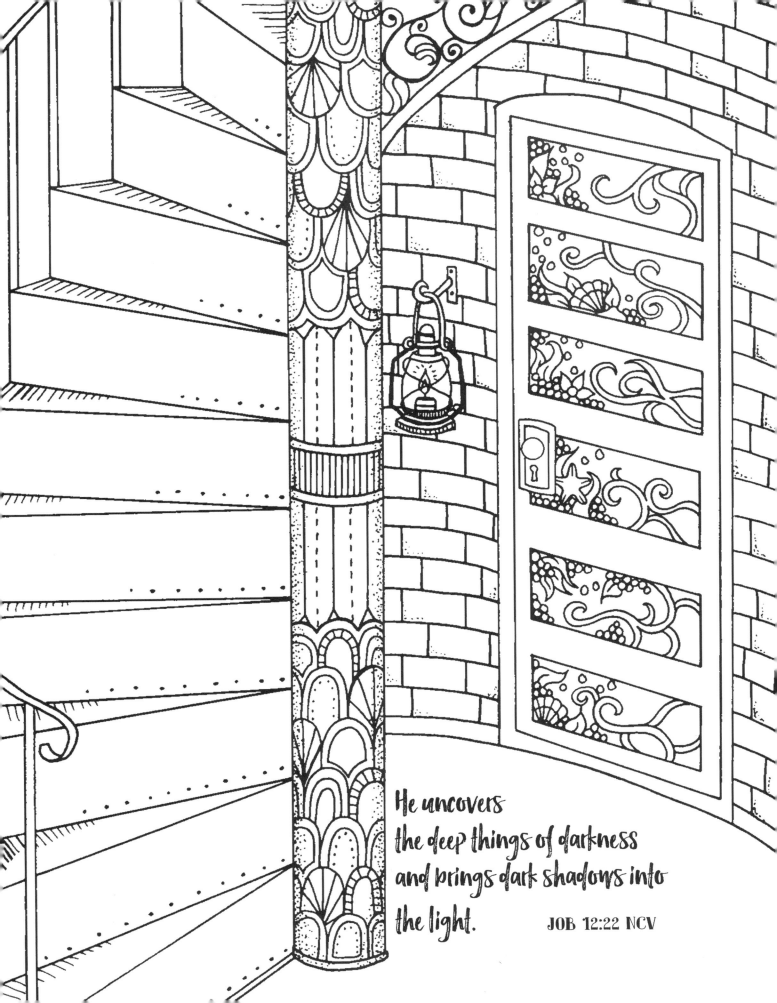

He uncovers
the deep things of darkness
and brings dark shadows into
the light. JOB 12:22 NCV

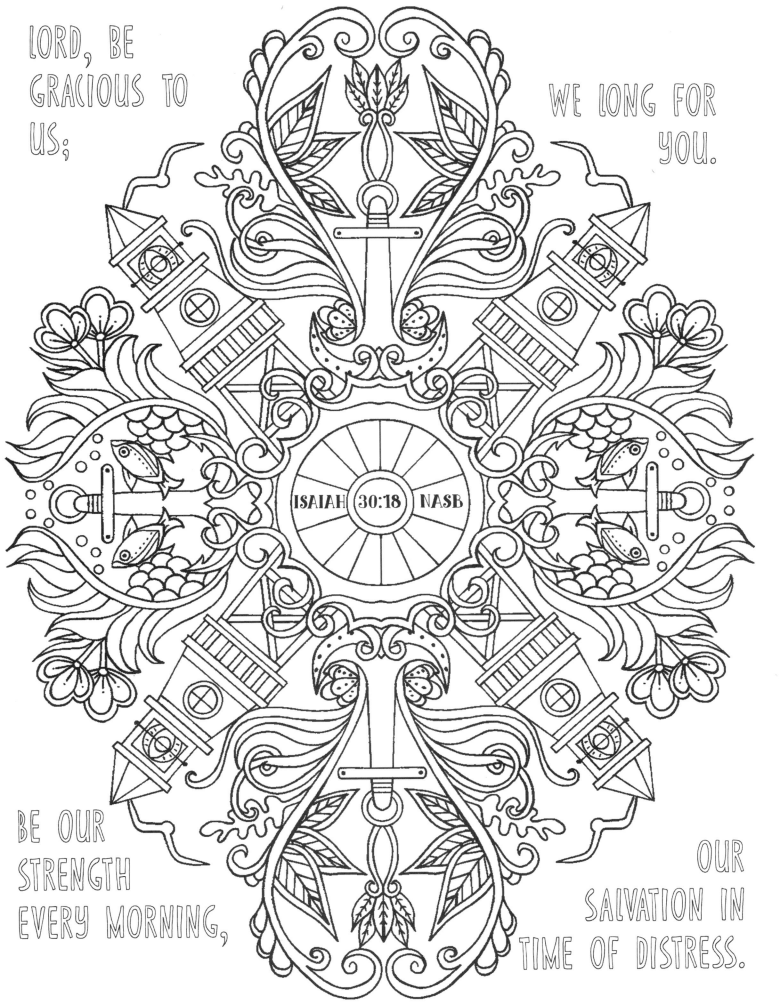

LORD, BE GRACIOUS TO US;

WE LONG FOR YOU.

ISAIAH 30:18 NASB

BE OUR STRENGTH EVERY MORNING,

OUR SALVATION IN TIME OF DISTRESS.

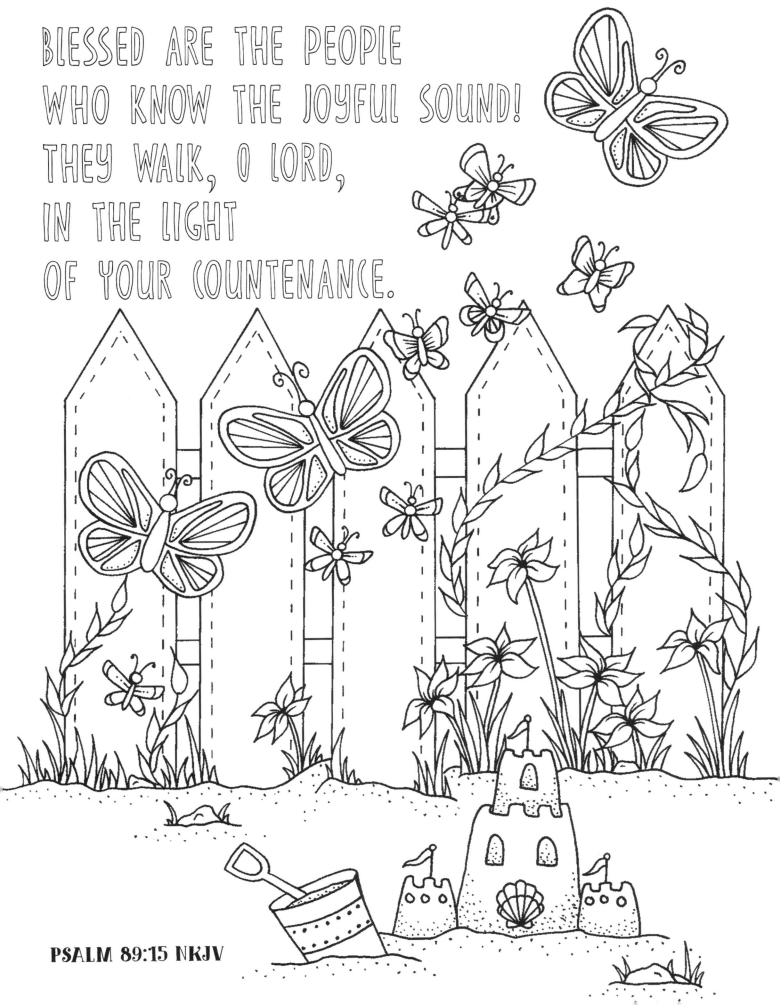

BLESSED ARE THE PEOPLE
WHO KNOW THE JOYFUL SOUND!
THEY WALK, O LORD,
IN THE LIGHT
OF YOUR COUNTENANCE.

PSALM 89:15 NKJV

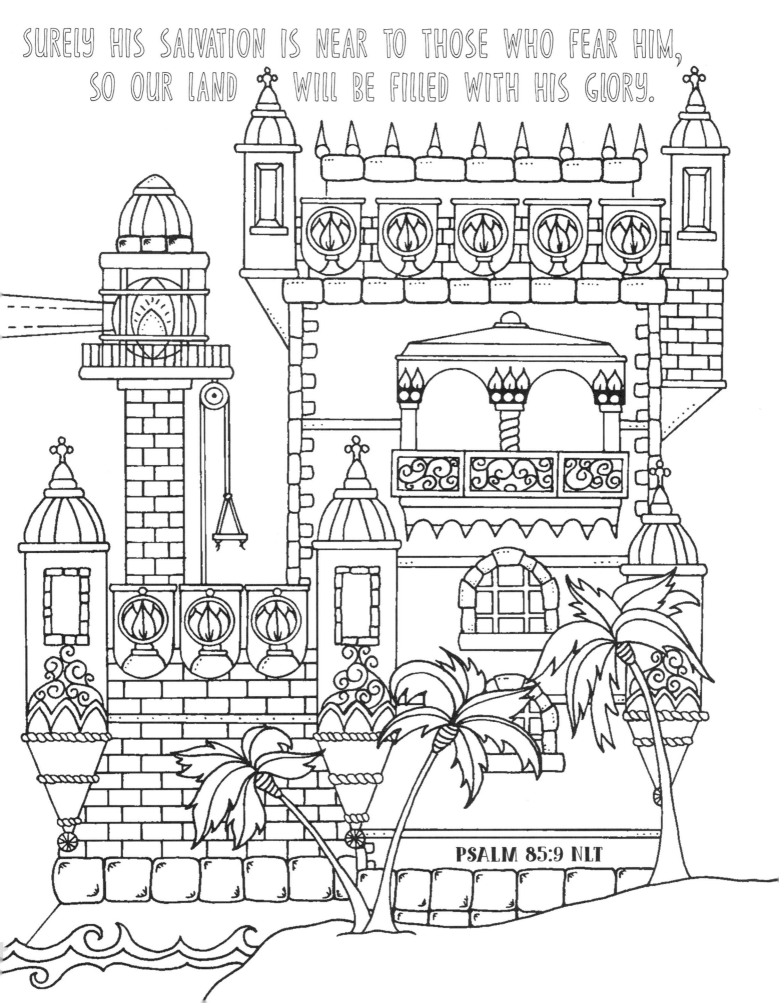

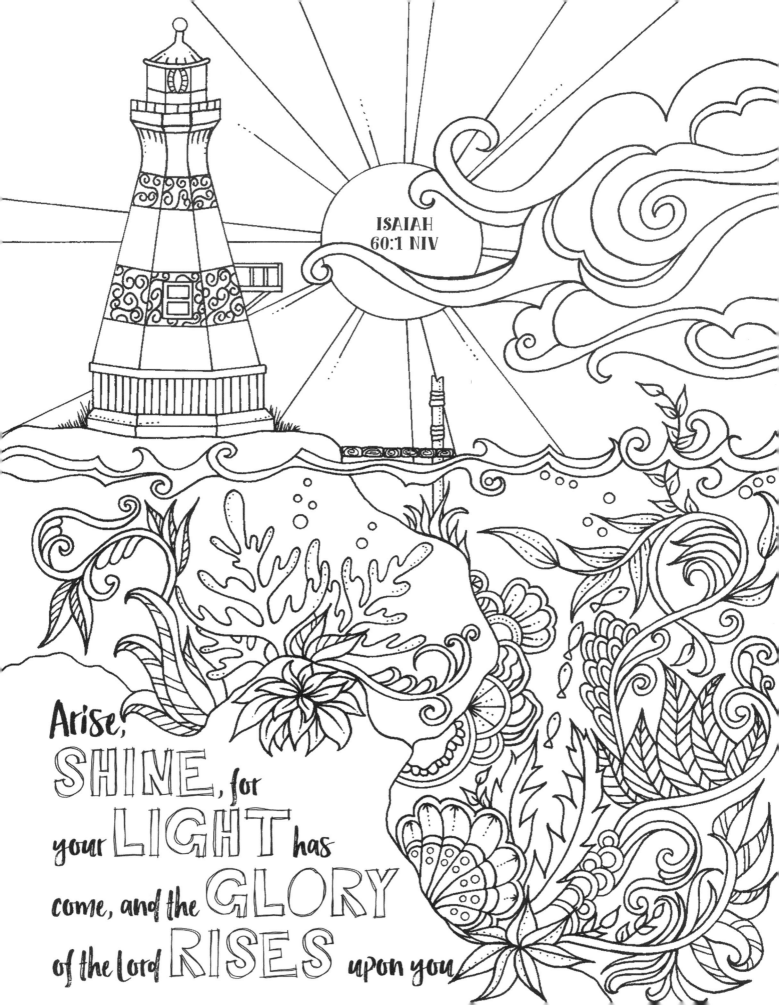

ISAIAH 60:1 NIV

Arise, SHINE, for your LIGHT has come, and the GLORY of the Lord RISES upon you

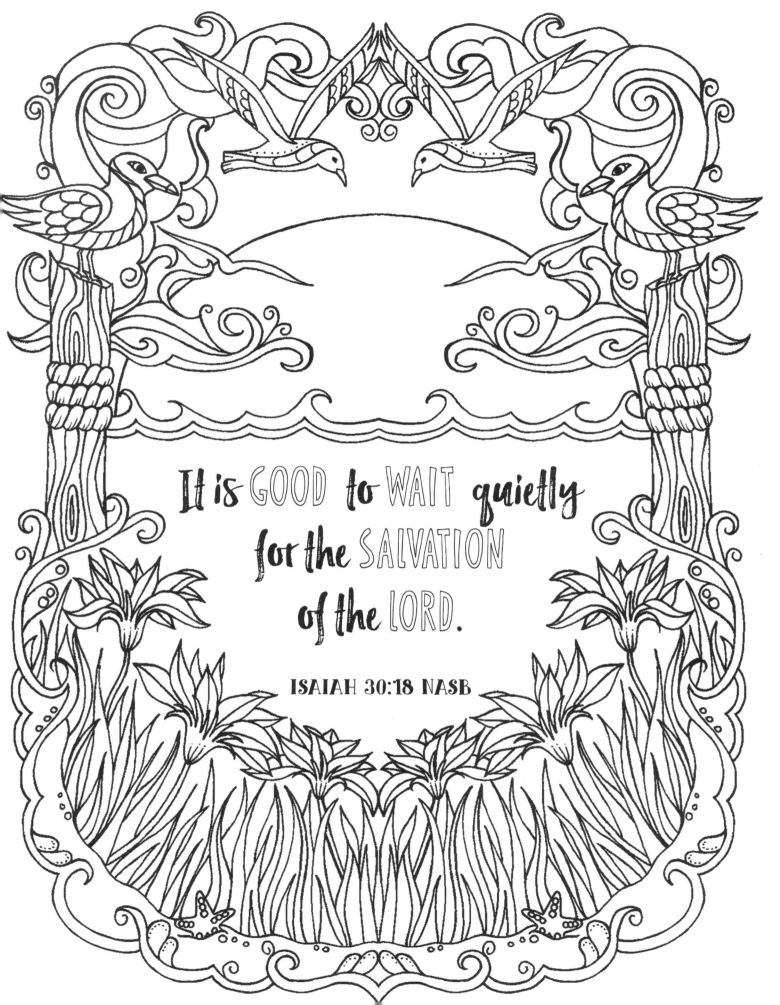

It is GOOD to WAIT quietly
for the SALVATION
of the LORD.

ISAIAH 30:18 NASB

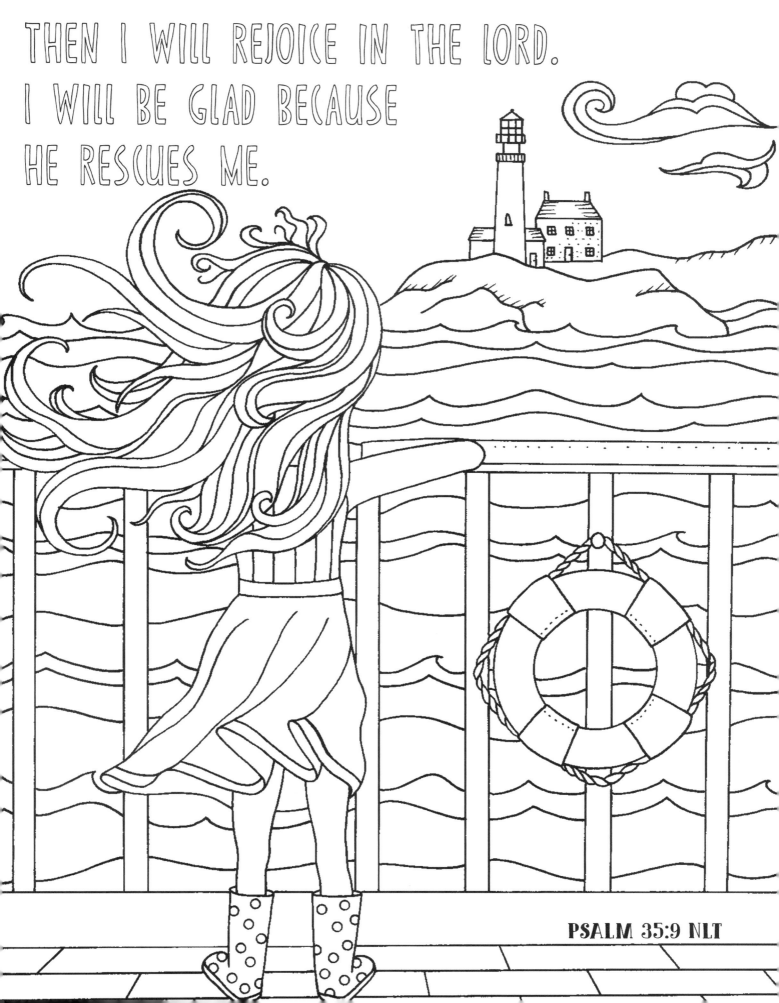

your WORD

is a LAMP to my feet

PSALM 119:105 NKJV

and a LIGHT

to my PATH.

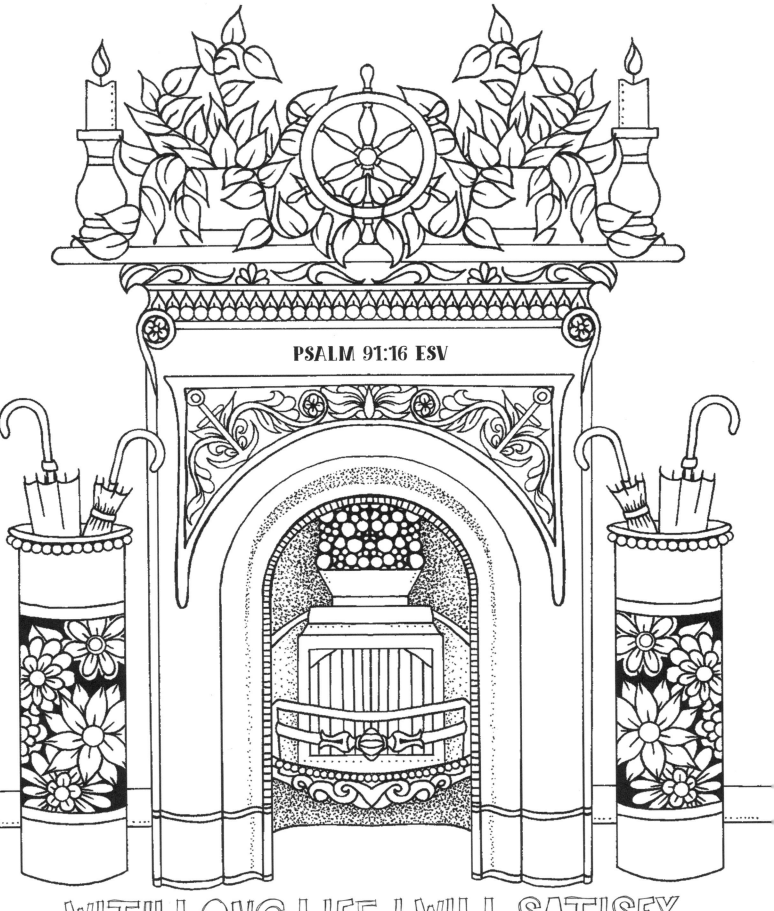

PSALM 91:16 ESV

WITH LONG LIFE I WILL SATISFY
HIM AND SHOW HIM MY SALVATION.

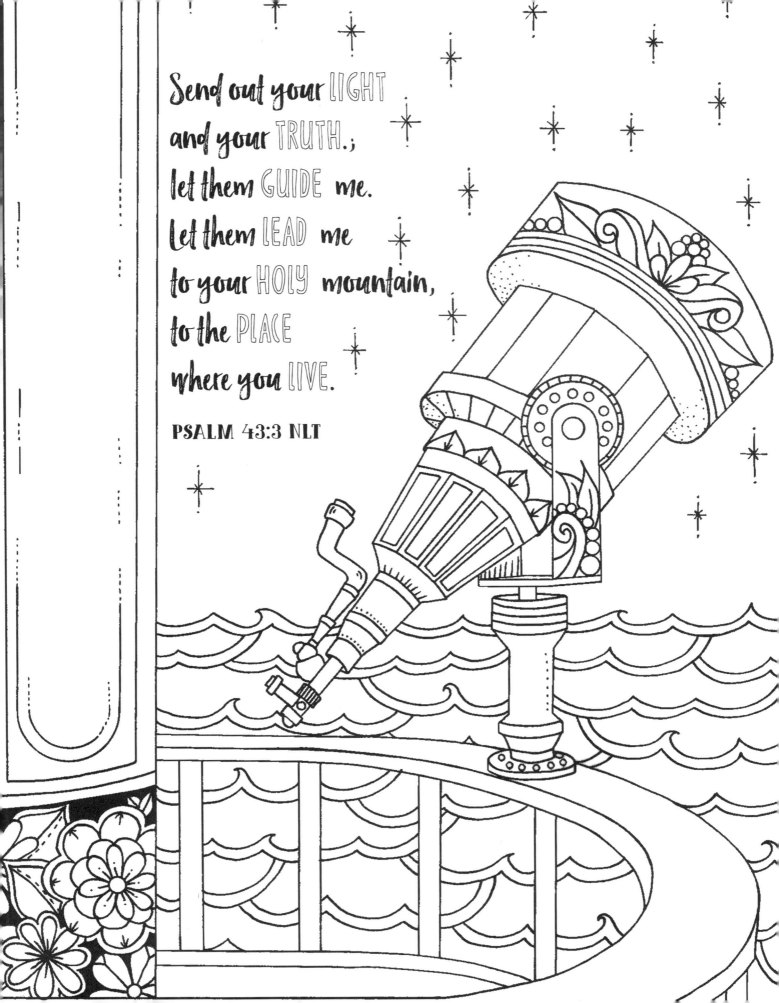

Send out your LIGHT and your TRUTH.; let them GUIDE me. Let them LEAD me to your HOLY mountain, to the PLACE where you LIVE.

PSALM 43:3 NLT

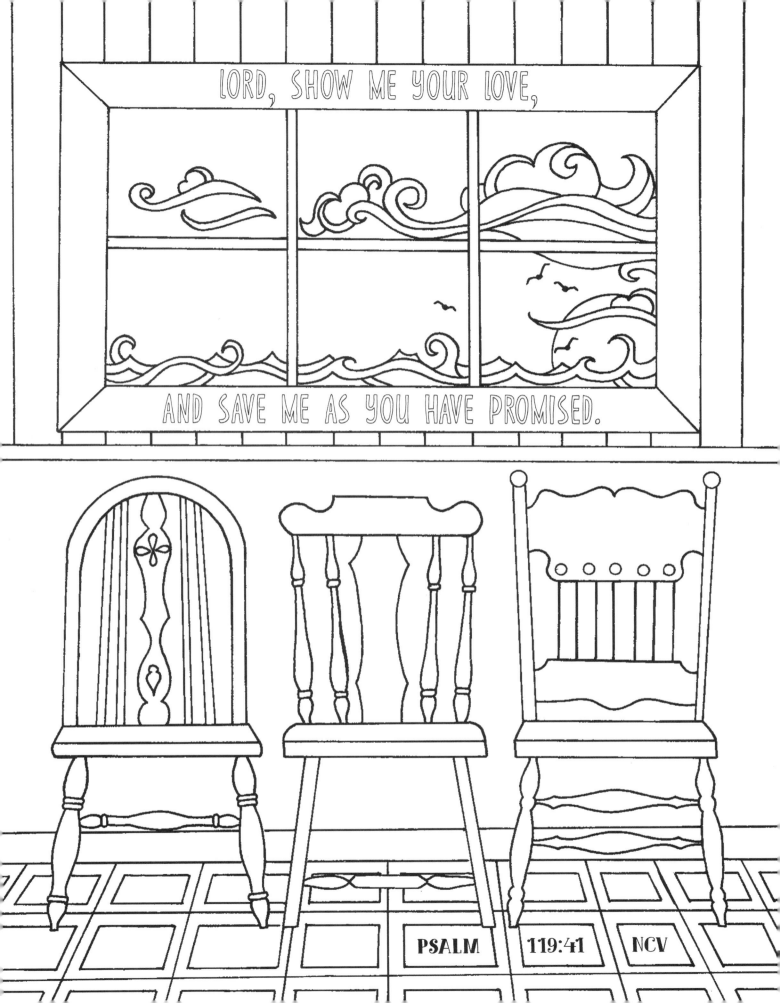

"I am the light of the world.

Whoever follows me will not walk in darkness,
but will have the light of life." JOHN 8:12 ESV

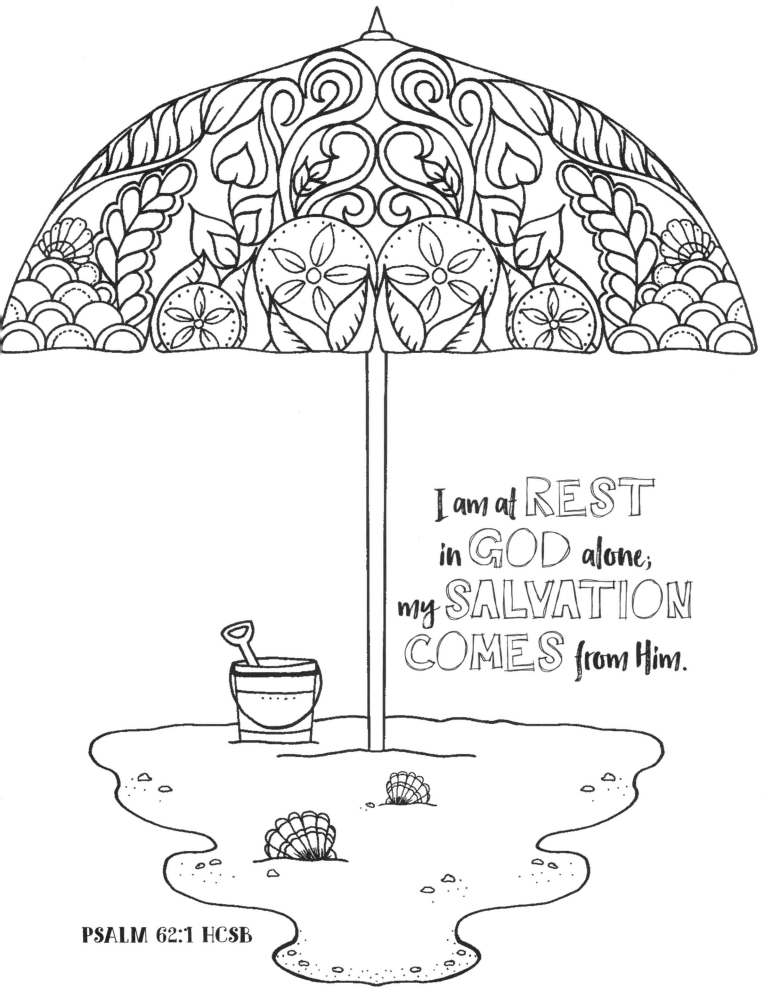

I am at REST
in GOD alone;
my SALVATION
COMES from Him.

PSALM 62:1 HCSB

RESTORE TO ME THE JOY OF YOUR SALVATION AND GRANT ME A WILLING SPIRIT, TO SUSTAIN ME.

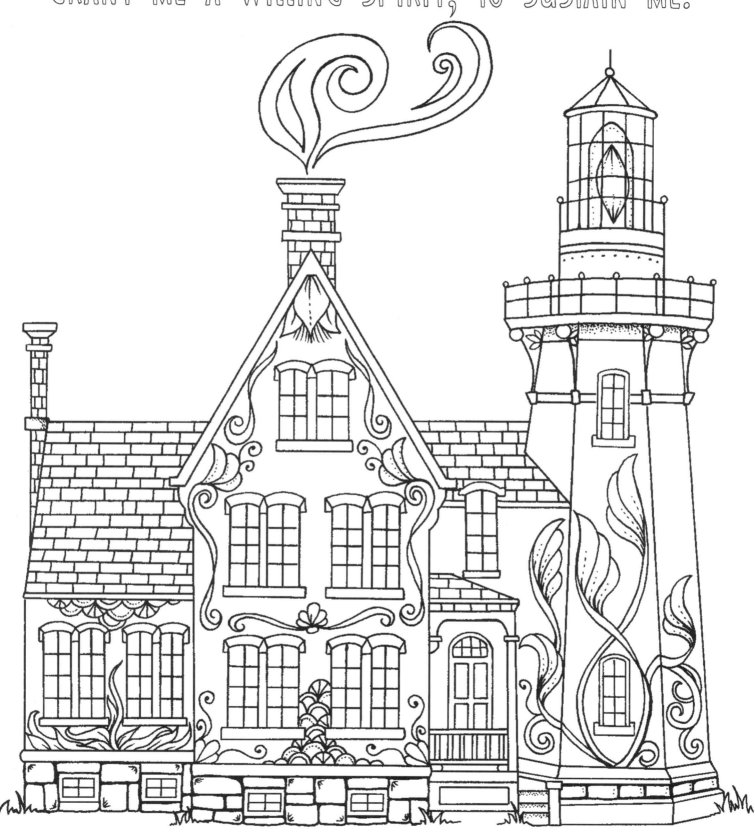

PSALM 51:12 NIV

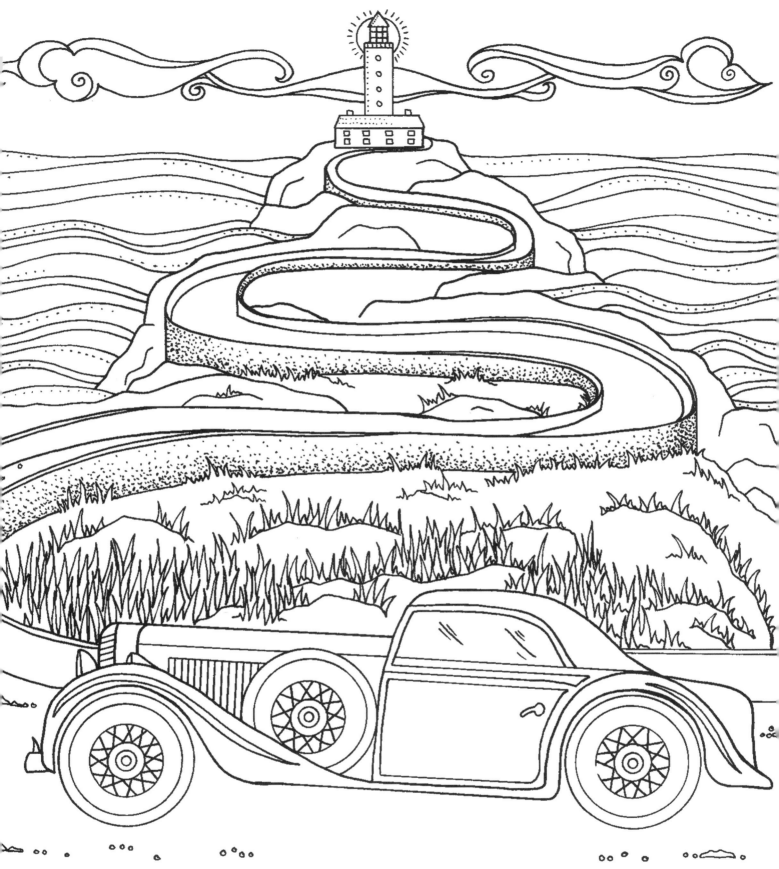

THE PATH OF THE RIGHTEOUS IS LIKE THE LIGHT OF DAWN,
WHICH SHINES BRIGHTER AND BRIGHTER UNTIL THE FULL DAY.
PROVERBS 4:18 ESV

LORD,
YOU LIGHT
MY LAMP;
MY GOD
ILLUMINATES
MY
DARKNESS.

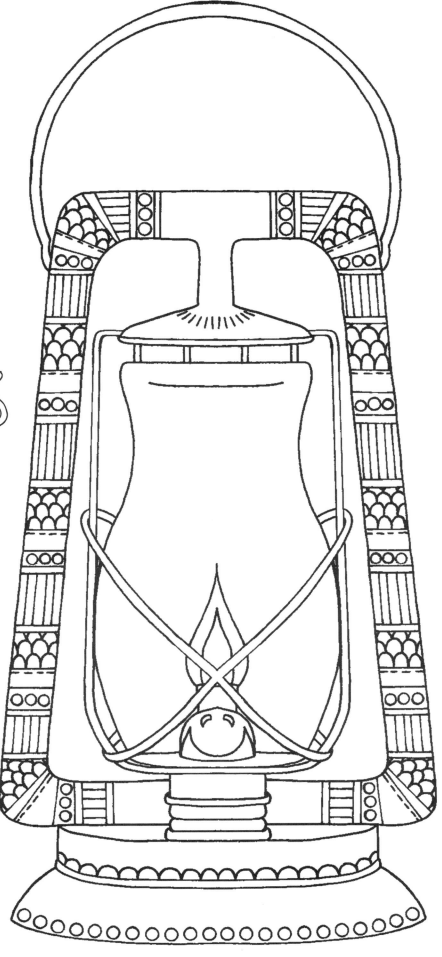

PSALM 18:28 HCSB

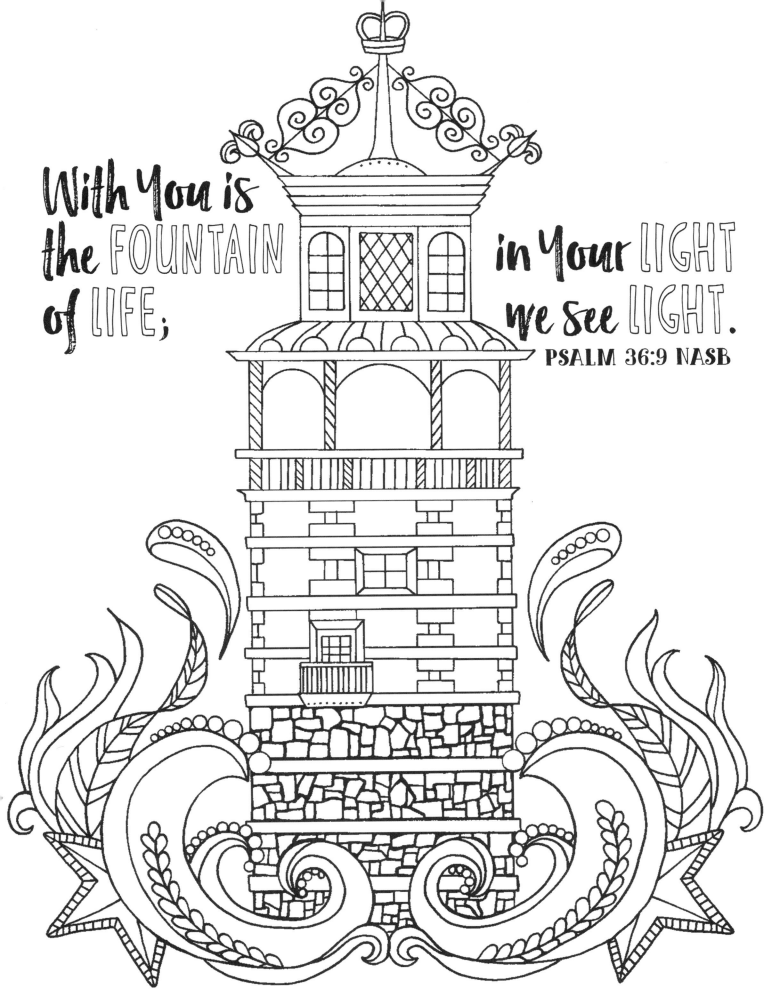

With You is the FOUNTAIN of LIFE; in Your LIGHT we see LIGHT.
PSALM 36:9 NASB

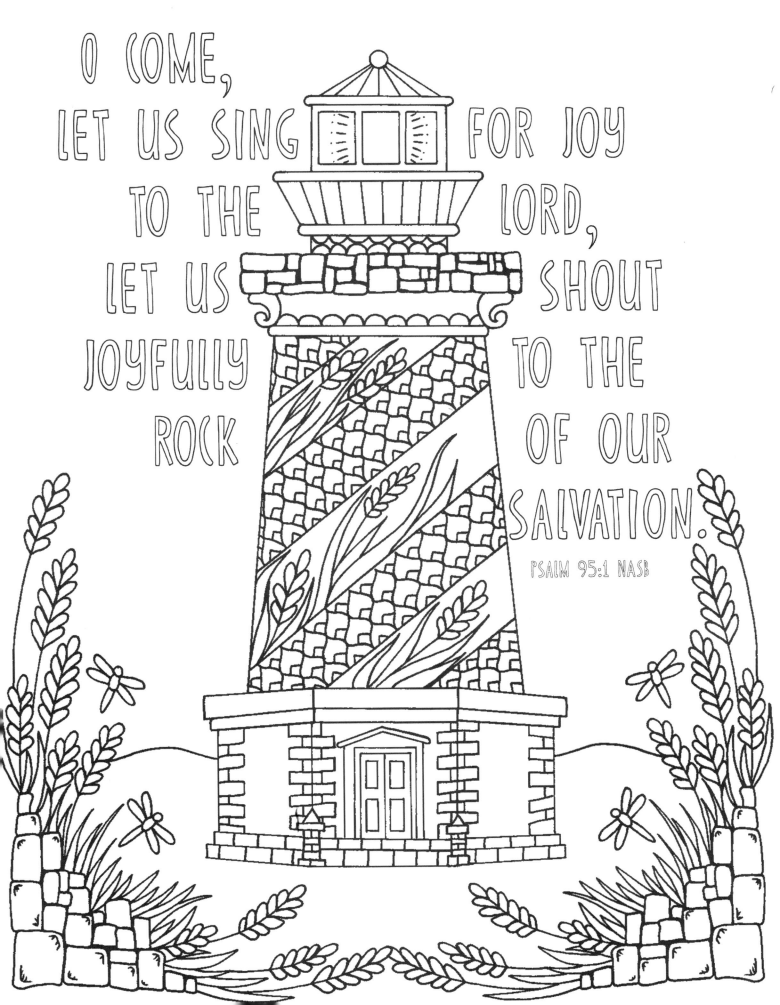

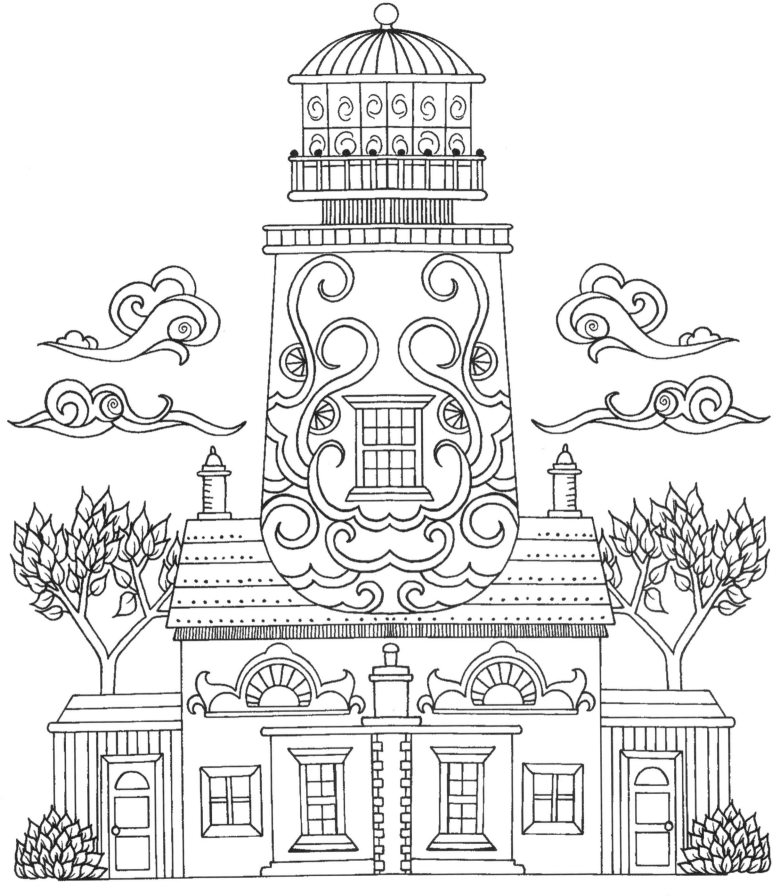

Light shines on the righteous and joy on the upright in heart.

PSALM 97:11 NIV

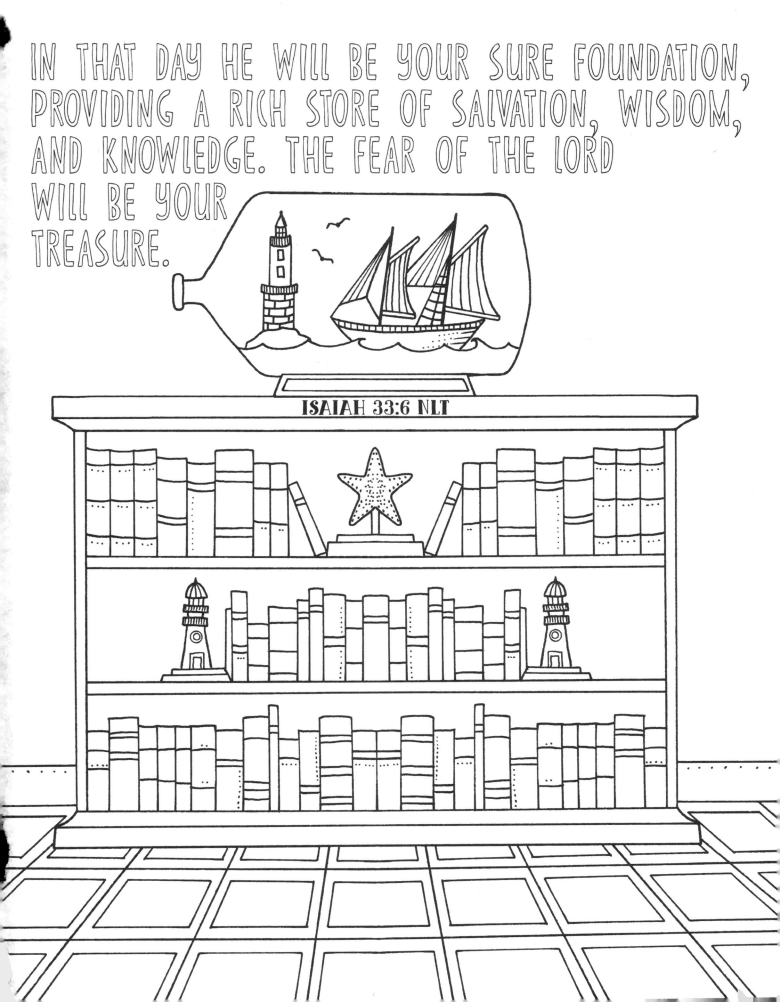

IN THAT DAY HE WILL BE YOUR SURE FOUNDATION, PROVIDING A RICH STORE OF SALVATION, WISDOM, AND KNOWLEDGE. THE FEAR OF THE LORD WILL BE YOUR TREASURE.

ISAIAH 33:6 NLT